BURN
YOUR
RESUME™

How to Ignite Your Exceptional Career

Taylor –
Good luck to you
@ the V of A.
I hope this book
is helpful as you
pursue BIG
goals for after
college.

Follow
us a
Facebook

Paul Frankenberg
& Ethan Dunham

Paul

E

Manufactured in the United States of America
First Edition, May 2012
Designed by Bruce Gore

Library of Congress Control Number: 2012907187

ISBN 978-0-9854-2700-9

CONTENTS

ACKNOWLEDGMENTS

WE WOULD LIKE TO THANK several people who have supported and inspired us in writing this book.

Paul would like to thank:

My wife, Beth: Thank you for your rock-solid support. I appreciate your encouragement in both starting Focus Search Partners and in writing this book. I love you.

Ethan (a.k.a., "E-MAN"): This book would not have been written without you. Thank you. To Jill and Amelia, thank you for your support during the long nights and busy weekends when "E" and I were discussing and writing this book.

Mom and Dad: Thank you Mom for teaching me the magic of books and for leading the way as the family's first author. Thank you Dad for your business advice and internet marketing leadership, which has been, and will continue to be, extremely helpful. I love you both. www.read-aloud-magic.com and www.ebiz-marketing-coach.com

Ethan would like to thank:

Jill and Amelia: Thank you for your support, encouragement, patience, love, insight, understanding, commentary, and never-ending faith in me. I love you both. You challenge me to be a better person and you have made this book possible.

My family: Mom, Dad, Bill, Kathleen, Cassie, Judd, Tricia and Mugsy—Thank you for cheering me on to the end. You have added incredible insight to the book, given brilliant advice and supported me without hesitation. I love you all and I know I wouldn't be who I am or where I am without you.

To Beth: Thank you for your grace and generosity throughout this process! You bring ease with you wherever you go, and have been a wonderful support to us.

To Paul: Through this project, you have become more a brother than a friend, more a friend than a collaborator. "All [you] do is add value." Thank you for toiling with me on this important work.

The authors would like to thank:

Jen Veal: We appreciate your writer's eye and insights in helping us produce an easy to read and well-written book. Thank you. www.youroutdoorfamily.com

Bruce Gore: We are humbled by your brilliance and your willingness to work with us. You have produced book covers for several of the most successful books in publication today and we believe you've provided us with a world-class product. Thank you. www.GoreStudio.com

College Students: We have talked with many of you locally and across the country, and we want to thank you for engaging with us, reading our manuscript and offering your suggestions. We are energized by your passions and goals, and we are thrilled to work with you to provide advice and direction in your career search.

" It is not the critic who counts;

not the man who points out how the strong man stumbles, or where the doer of deeds could have done them better. The credit belongs to the man who is actually in the arena, whose face is marred by dust and sweat and blood; who strives valiantly; who errs, who comes short again and again, because there is no effort without error and shortcoming; but who does actually strive to do the deeds; who knows great enthusiasms, the great devotions; who spends himself in a worthy cause; who at the best knows in the end the triumph of high achievement, and who at the worst, if he fails, at least fails while daring greatly, so that his place shall never be with those cold and timid souls who neither know victory nor defeat."

—THEODORE ROOSEVELT

PREFACE

"I have learned that if one advances confidently in the direction of his dreams, and endeavors to live the life he has imagined, he will meet with success unexpected in common hours."

—HENRY DAVID THOREAU

BURN YOUR RESUME. It's time to determine your career path and take action. The job search of the 21st century is an insider's game: many of the same rules apply, but the stakes are higher and the competition is tougher. This is a new world, a new economy and a new employment landscape, and you have to stand out from a pack of people just like you.

Now, more than ever before, you have to thread the needle at the right time, in the right place and with the right people for the right opportunity.... Otherwise, you could find yourself five or 10 years into a career you never wanted, making less money than you wanted and without a plan to get back on track. Relying only on a resume, cover letter and an interview just doesn't cut it anymore—especially for freshly minted college graduates.

Now is the time to Burn Your Resume, make your moves and ignite your career. It's easy for people to tell you what to do but how to do it is the challenge. This book will provide you with the how-to for igniting your exceptional career.

In spite of our title, we don't intend for anyone to literally set flame to their resume. Rather, we want the incendiary image to drive you in new directions. Imagine burning your resume and then identify the image it brings to mind: something enticing, powerful and consuming, to erase the old methods and to pursue a new path with energy, focus and confidence. Burn your resume to relieve yourself of your exclusive dependence on it. Recreate it to tell your story rather than allowing it to dictate your story. We hope you will be inspired by the image and metaphor of burning your resume, and will reorient and commit your resources toward action on your own behalf. This book will assist you in distinguishing yourself from your competition and will fuel your professional advancement.

It is clear that many smart, motivated and ambitious college graduates don't actually know how to actively manage the building blocks of identifying, pursuing and launching a successful career. You may have heard that you need to "network." We will teach you how to do it successfully. Additionally, you will be shown how to find your career passions, identify strong networking contacts, develop a clear and professional resume, prepare correctly for an outstanding interview, negotiate your offer and start your career on a rock-solid foundation. This is all easily said, but the how-to is not taught in practical formats—especially not in college. *Burn Your Resume* is your key to a future that outpaces your peers and sets you apart from the very moment you start taking action. This book is a user-friendly field manual that offers examples and instructions for each crucial move in igniting your exceptional career.

We are excited to offer you this practical field guide—a playbook—to help you identify, pursue and launch your career, aligned with your talents and passions. In order to proactively manage an exceptional career, you will need to identify and align your skills (what you naturally do well), your passions (what you care most deeply about) and your interests (what you find most engaging or fascinating) with your networking advantages (the people you know who are in positions of influence), your resources (professors, friends, family, career centers, advisors and alumni databases) and market demand. Over time, you will personalize your resume and messaging based on your style, who you are and who you want to be. Our intention is to help set you on an uncommon path to opportunity and achievement.

This book is a how-to guide for transitioning from the classroom to your career. You'll have to practice, and you will have to change old habits and develop new ones. In the 1992 letter to the shareholders of Berkshire Hathaway, Warren Buffett shared a lesson he learned from a golf pro: "Practice makes permanent." That is the philosophy you should employ every time you put this book down: set a goal, develop a plan, utilize resources, take ownership and act. Take the time to reflect on, plan, practice and execute the points we've drawn up for you throughout this book and you will be able to seize the opportunities you desire.

Learning how to do something takes time, effort and focus. For your benefit, we have set the guideposts and laid the foundation for your career search. Your job is to execute, execute, execute. So, Burn Your Resume. Determine your passion, take action each day for what you intend the next day to be, and launch your career. Take that first step. Start at the first page and we will help you cross the bridge from college to career.

We look forward to personally interacting with you and providing additional insights, guidance and practical advice as you pursue and develop your exceptional career.

Paul Frankenberg   &   Ethan Dunham

INTRODUCTION

The Champion's Margin

"Before I got in the ring, I'd have already won or lost it out on the road. The real part is won or lost somewhere far away from the witnesses—behind the lines, in the gym and out there on the road long before I dance under those lights."

—MUHAMMAD ALI

"THE CHAMPION'S MARGIN" is a differentiator. It's what sets you apart. It's the small stuff you do to separate yourself, to initiate and develop an exceptional career. In sports, you hear about it all the time: the extra effort, the lean at the race's finish line, the reach for the wall of the pool that yields the fractions of seconds separating first from second, the champion from the runner-up. Achieving The Champion's Margin depends on your work, effort, investment and willingness to try, fail and try again.

An anonymous source gives clarity to The Champion's Margin: "Some men can run the fastest, jump the highest, or lift the heaviest, but no man has the corner on ambition, desire and hustle." Ambition, desire and hustle are key components of The Champion's Margin, and they dovetail with our instructions on how to become an outstanding candidate for the job of your choice. The Champion's Margin is a cohesive series of steps that will make you distinct within your peer group.

Managing and cultivating an exceptional career depends on the things we mention above, because separating yourself from the rest of your peer group requires an unwavering commitment to take the next step. There is no glory in not trying, and this holds true for the exercises we've created, the advice we will continue to provide and the plans you will execute from this book. This is The Champion's Margin.

LEADERSHIP AND THE CHAMPION'S MARGIN

Legendary management consultant Peter Drucker described leadership as follows: "Leadership is not magnetic personality—that can just as well be a glib tongue. It is not 'making friends and influencing people'—that is flattery. Leadership is lifting a person's vision to higher sights, the raising of a person's performance to a higher standard, the building of a personality beyond its normal limitations." As the leader of your own future, it is up to you to lift your own vision to higher sights, to raise your own performance to a higher standard and to build your own personality beyond its normal limitations.

Some people would have you believe that a leader is always on stage. If that's true, it makes sense to spend time thinking about how to make yourself stand out positively from your competition. Other people would have you believe that the best leaders are quietly in command, facilitating others' success subtly and without fanfare. If that's true, it makes sense to spend time thinking about how to make yourself competent to the point of powerful influence. Either way, you need clear and well-developed aspirations in order to define and shape who you are and who you want to be.

Fundamentals remain consistent through history, in spite of the incredible technological and sociological developments that have been taking place over the last 50 years. Think about sports, music, banking and even baking, and you'll come to the same conclusion: everything is built upon fundamentals (the jump shot, the eighth note, supply and demand and the activation of yeast, for example). The foundation is what supports innovation and evolution. The following four practices will separate you from the field:

Be Punctual

If you are early, you're on time. If you are on time, you're late. Nothing ruins opportunity or reputation faster than tardiness, so pack up the night before and prepare a to-do list to ensure you are ready to go. Drive the route to your meeting or your interview ahead of time, especially if you've never been to the meeting location before, and account for traffic. Know where to park and how to get in the front door. Pack your briefcase or portfolio with notes, materials and questions.

Your goal is to be 5 to 10 minutes early to interviews and meetings. If you are too early, you run the risk of creating an awkward situation or pressure for the meeting host. In the event that you have an unavoidable delay, call and give an honest assessment of your estimated time of arrival. This shows courtesy and awareness, as well as professionalism.

The bottom line is to be at an appointment when you have committed to be there. If an interviewer has to wonder where you are, you have missed the opportunity to create a positive impression.

Be Polite

Good manners will never count against you. However, bad manners can cost you a shot at an opportunity, whether that's an appointment or first date, a meeting with an alumnus or possible career advocate, or an interview with a would-be dream boss for a dream job.

If you are meeting at an office, greet the receptionist and take time to ask how his or her day is going. Stand up when your host comes to greet you. Offer a firm, confident handshake and make comfortable eye contact with a smile. Say "please" and "thank you" when you are given something to drink. Send a handwritten note of thanks to people who take time out of their day to meet or speak with you.

Politeness will help you to form a positive reputation as you move through the networking, relationship-building and interviewing processes.

Be Prepared

Do your research. Understand the backgrounds of the people you meet. Be aware of industry trends, an organization's strengths and weaknesses, and current events that may affect an organization.

It is important to ask questions during an interview. If you pass on the chance to ask questions, you may as well pass on the relationship, role, contact or opportunity itself. There is nothing that turns off a colleague, teammate or interviewer faster than a candidate who lacks curiosity about the organization or the competitive landscape. If you are in an interview and pass on the chance to ask questions, be prepared to pass on the opportunity itself. The interview is about building rapport, presenting yourself as a viable candidate who is easy to envision in the role, and alleviating some of the pressure and risk from the interviewer. Do not give them reason to say, "I can't see you in this role."

Be Present

Don't allow yourself to be distracted by other responsibilities during a meeting. From the moment you arrive, your attention should be undivided. Turn off your phone, take notes, ask questions and build dialogue. Give a potential employer your full attention and invest in the experience of getting to know the environment, teammates, client and culture.

Hiring managers across the board agree that their task is to comfortably envision a candidate in the role. Be a great listener. Make the person sitting across from you feel your focus and attention. Be present.

CHAPTER 1

Make College Work for You

"We set young leaders up for a fall if we encourage them to envision what they can do before they consider the kind of person they should be."

—RUTH BARTON

For THIS FIRST STEP, take a few minutes to think back to your college selection process. Choosing your college was a living simulation of the approach to research, preparation, critical thinking and personal presentation you will develop and use for the rest of your career.

When you decided where to attend college, you presumably made your decision based on varying factors: where your friends were going; somewhere your family could afford; where *U.S. News & World Report* said you should go; where you could get a scholarship or playing time; the school where your boyfriend or girlfriend had chosen to go; somewhere you could enjoy specific geography or city size; where the rest of your family has gone; or where you were accepted. Few people choose a college based on a specific curriculum or career pursuit.

Once you entered college, you began to expand and develop your interests and passions and built specific career plans around those interests and passions.

We do not expect you to know today where you want to be

in ten or twenty years. One of the greatest aspects of youth is the ability to have multiple interests, and you need to know that your career will evolve as you develop personally. This is normal. Don't feel like you have to over-plan your entire career. As Adam Bryant says in his book, *The Corner Office*, "Prepare for a career, don't plan it." We simply want you to be thoughtful in starting your career so that you are following your passions, skills and interests ... and not just accepting what is coming at you.

Thinking through your college experience and aligning that with your career goals is the first step in setting the course of your career. Think specifically about why you chose to attend your college or university, who you are becoming, what you have done as a student, where you have succeeded, where you have struggled, what you have enjoyed the most and what you have learned about yourself. You can weave these answers together to tell your story.

This is a process, which requires reflection and action. Here are a few questions to ask yourself as you get started:

1. Who do you want to become?
   * *Identify and think about your talents.*
2. In college, what is or has been your favorite subject?
   * *Identify and pursue your passion.*
3. What are you doing in your extracurricular activities?
   * *Identify what you most enjoy working on, what you're learning, the people with whom you are working and interacting, and what you're being exposed to.*

4. What is your college or university known for? What are their particularly strong programs?

  - *If their top programs are not your focus area, be prepared to find strengths in your own path to pursue with passion.*

5. Who on the faculty, alumni, or your advisor might serve as a strong advocate or mentor for your career preparation?

  - *Who at your school knows you well enough to give you an edge as you approach your launch into "the real world"?*

  - *Many professors are thrilled to assist their current and recent students in career search and management. Identify and develop those connections.*

It is important to recognize and utilize the resources in a college setting that remain at your disposal: academic departments, staff, offices and networks. Spend time figuring out how to leverage your university's resources to meet your career development needs.

Your college or university career management center (CMC) can be a terrific resource. However, this resource is like any other worthwhile endeavor: without ongoing investment, there can be no payout.

Visit the CMC and ask for a tour. That first visit should serve as an orientation to the resources at your disposal: the CMC team, corporate networks, alumni connections, internship opportunities and general recommended timelines. Make sure you set aside an hour for this first meeting and be clear about the agenda: "I'm here to learn about the career management center. May I get some help figuring out how to make the most of my time here?"

After touring the CMC, sit down with a career counselor or set up an appointment within one week to follow up if that isn't possible. During the meeting, go through the following checklist, write down the results and plan weekly, monthly, quarterly and annual milestones. Map your trajectory. Then follow through. The follow-through is The Champion's Margin here and throughout every aspect of this book. John Wooden, arguably the greatest college basketball coach ever, once said, "Failure to prepare is preparing to fail." When it comes to getting exactly what you want, this is all the more true about follow-through. We suggest you use this list of questions and tasks to frame your visit to the career center:

- Do I have a clear idea of the type(s) of career I want to pursue? If not, ask the counselor to help you find an internship, part-time job, or college-based opportunity with a small business.
- What professional or technical resources are at my disposal through the CMC?
- Beyond technical resources, does the school offer career counseling to help students get a better sense of career paths based on their strengths and interests?
- What do I need to do before graduation to best position myself for the career I want?

- What should I be thinking about at this point in my career search?
- Where should I be looking for information on a variety of career paths?
- What companies have strong relationships with our college or university?
- Which internship programs do you recommend or suggest I apply to?
- Do alumni help students with career searches or offer internship opportunities?
- What have your most successful students done to stand out from the crowd and seize their opportunity of choice?

THINGS TO CONSIDER:

- Be true to your core values, beliefs and who you want to be throughout your career search.
- Be prepared to talk about and discuss job-related experiences you have enjoyed or have been exposed to.
- Ask what knowledge, skills, abilities and experiences are crucial to landing an internship or job.
- Ask for suggestions about careers that utilize the same or similar skill sets.
- Schedule a follow-up appointment with your career counselor.

YOUR CHAMPION'S MARGIN TAKEAWAY(S):

_____

_____

_____

_____

_____

_____

_____

_____

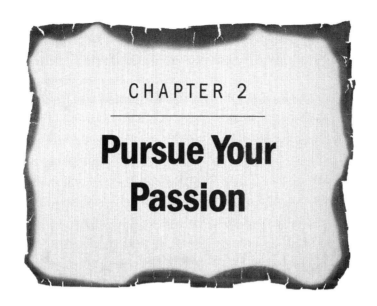

CHAPTER 2

Pursue Your Passion

"There is no passion to be found in playing small—in settling for a life that is less than the one you are capable of living."

—NELSON MANDELA

Robert Iger, president and chief executive officer of The Walt Disney Company, is known for his great admiration for curious and passionate people. "Passionate curiosity is indispensable, no matter what the job is," Iger said. "You want somebody who is just alert and very awake and engaged with the world and wanting to know more. Top executives who are passionately curious can also spot like-minded people from a mile away."

When you begin to forge your career plan, start by thinking of the ultimate goals that you have in mind. By establishing clear, concrete, lofty and admirable goals for your career—a plan or a set of objectives—you are establishing a foundation that will differentiate you from your peers.

Mary Kay Ash, founder of Mary Kay Cosmetics, said: "Don't limit yourself. Many people limit themselves to what they think they can achieve. You can go as far as your mind lets you."

Determine the steps you need to take today in anticipation of what you envision your future to be. Too many people allow themselves to be passive participants in life, school, jobs, relationships, health management and so on. Be proactive in defining and building your own career.

On the Oprah Winfrey show in 1997, actor and comedian Jim Carrey revealed, "Long before my movie career had really taken off, I wrote myself a check for 10 million dollars for 'acting services rendered' and gave myself 5 years and dated it Thanksgiving 1995. I put it in my wallet and kept it there, and it deteriorated and deteriorated. And then, just before Thanksgiving 1995, I found out I was going to make 10 million dollars on Dumb & Dumber."

What is your metaphorical payday going to be? Most importantly, how do you plan to get there?

HARNESSING YOUR PASSION

Passion is a critical word in life. In fact, it's the clarion call of the 21st century. We wrote this book to encourage you to identify and take action to pair your passions with your career. You may pursue something because you want to earn certain dollar amount or think it's the best way to start your career. However, if your choices are misaligned with your natural talents and passions, we believe that you will soon find yourself unhappy with your role and perhaps your company. We are suggesting that you identify and pursue those things you care most about, the things that make you who you are, or the things that get you out of bed in the morning.

Let's talk about "dream" jobs. There are so many industries, employers, roles, entrepreneurial opportunities and needs in the world that there must be a job that will allow you to optimize your own potential. You should dream, define, pursue and land the job and career you want.

Few people understand that hiring managers see a person only as that person represents him or herself. The person screening your application is often making decisions based on concrete and specific criteria, through which your passions may not be readily apparent. You have to make your experience, interests and skills align with the hiring company, with a focus toward results. Don't assume anyone knows or can imagine anything about you and what you offer. It is your job to educate them and to make yourself an easy hiring decision.

Ethan's Story:

Ethan needed to learn how to navigate the job-search landscape before defining his career. Just prior to launching his job search, he realized that he was expecting too great a portion of the job search process to simply work for him.

Ethan was well educated and had strong recommendations, experience and a powerful resume. He knew what he could offer a company, but initially he didn't understand the variables at play when he saw others landing the roles he wanted. He quickly learned that education alone is not the only path to success.

Once Ethan realized that he needed to take charge and manage those variables, he began to make some progress. He learned to translate his experience, skills, passions, strengths and interests into language that prospective employers could understand and appreciate. He prepared for challenges inherent in the job-search process. He also began to understand networking and career progression, as well as how to make himself stand out among his peers.

It is important for you to remember that the hiring manager is under great pressure to make the right decision. The cost of a bad hire is significant—a multiple of the individual's annual compensation. Put yourself in the shoes of the people considering you. What concerns do they have? What pressure are they feeling? What are they looking for? When you take the time to consider their perspective, you will find that you can tailor your points of emphasis and messaging to more effectively represent yourself as a viable and desirable candidate. Make yourself an easy hiring decision.

Ethan was ultimately able to reframe his resume and organize the written and verbal messages he was sending in order to be an easy-hire candidate. By shaping each explanatory bullet into "situation, action, outcome," there was less need for interpretation. His target—a dream opportunity that would lay a foundation for his career—demanded certain skills, perspectives and experience; an approach to and philosophy about learning; and a team-orientation that resonated with the company. Through conducting industry and company research, interpreting position qualifications and responsibilities and surveying the company's values and direction on their website, he was able to communicate specific experiences on his resume, in his cover letter and throughout his interview process. Through his understanding of the role, the company, and the industry, he was able to position himself as an obvious choice for his current employer.

With that in mind, take action and be honest with yourself as you answer the following questions. The purpose of the following exercise is to help you identify your natural talents, skills, passions and interests without the pressure or criterion of external influence. You need to be able to be direct in identifying what drives you and what opportunities excite you. Be honest with yourself as you answer the following questions.

SELF-ASSESSMENT

Your honest answers to the following questions will reveal the things you actually enjoy doing. We call these "the hard questions" because sometimes it can be most difficult to admit certain things to ourselves about ourselves.

Now that you're clear on our expectations, apply the lesson. We're going to drive to the core of some issues that will help you determine where and in what setting you will be able to find the environment of best fit. You may find out that the answers to these questions also tell you where not to go, what not to do and what paths not to run down.

1. What are my natural talents?

We are all good at something. Individually, you have strengths and skills that stand out from your peers. One way to identify these outstanding traits is to look for the things you fall back on. What are your "go-to" skills, roles, jobs and so on? With group projects, are you the analyst, the marketer, the logistician or the researcher? Do you speak up in class as a thought leader or opinion leader, or do you sit in the back and watch the action? Are you driven to produce art or offer creative solutions to problems, or do you write computer programs for fun? As Henry David Thoreau said, "Pursue a path, however crooked and narrow, in which you can walk with love and reverence." So ask yourself, "What am I best at doing?" … And be secure enough to answer honestly.

Maybe you are a natural at making friends or organizing student clubs or events. Maybe you've never struggled with writing long papers or acing your math and science classes. Are you creative, a strong communicator, an organizer, a task-master, a strategist or a risk-taker?

Talents are often hard to identify because they rarely strike us as unique or out-of-the-ordinary. Be willing to ask those closest to you—friends, classmates, professors, work supervisors and family members—to help you identify your natural talents.

2. *What do I most enjoy doing?*

What if we can get paid to do something that is fun for us? In today's world, the work/life balance is a goal for many graduates and the ideal aim would be to find personal and professional fulfillment in the same place. Since you've picked up this book you're in on the secret: People should really enjoy their work. As the saying goes, "It's only work when there's something else you'd rather be doing." The most successful individuals we know have found a way to blend the personal with the professional, the work with the play. You owe it to yourself to pursue what comes naturally, what brings you joy, and to get paid for something that brings out the best in you. So ask yourself "What do I most enjoy doing?" ... And be bold enough to answer honestly.

3. *What motivates me?*

Knowledge? Demonstrating mastery of a topic? Quality of life? Relationships or transactions? Social and community issues or services? Entrepreneurial activities? Selling ideas or products? Organization and process? Money? Public recognition?

4. *If I could do anything professionally, what would it be?*

Push yourself beyond the safe threshold of "I guess I'll just _____" or "I don't know." What do you really want to do? This is different from the question, "What do my parents want me to do?" Be honest and take the time to think and talk with others to develop and evaluate ideas. If you have never set a goal, this is the time to understand what it means to set a goal. The process of goal setting will place you on a path moving forward.

5. *Is there something I cannot imagine NOT doing?*

If you are absolutely compelled to do something—cook, write, work in a lab, sell, research or build—then you should listen to your own voice. If there is something you cannot imagine NOT doing, start there. That is your passion.

6. *Is there a demand in the world for my natural skills and inclinations?*

Be honest with yourself about whether or not you can command any kind of compensation for your natural skills and inclinations. Does this job or career path exist? If not, is there an unmet need somewhere in the market? If the answer to either of those is "yes," then you've moved to the next level of your initial exploration. If the answer is "no," then perhaps it's time to reexamine your answers to the questions and exercises up to this point. If you find that one of your passions does not generate revenue, consider making it a hobby or a community volunteering effort and continue to evaluate your interests to find roles that can sustain your professional career.

7. *Can I get paid to follow my passion?*

Think through your primary passions to determine which one you should pursue as a career. You may have strong social service passions. While pursuing social services as a primary career is terrific, there are many ways to serve the greater good while also pursuing a career in another area. You can offer your expertise and skill sets to non-profit organizations, join a board of directors, volunteer for fundraising efforts, donate money and build a business impacting your chosen social service.

If you can't pay the rent, that's a problem. If you can't repay education loans, that's a problem. However, this need not be cause to squelch your dreams. Rather, it is all part of managing your career. If funding is going to be a potential problem, consider following an alternate passion or another pursuit that you can enjoy to achieve your goal. This will allow you to begin a career, while also building cash reserves and experience that may allow you to pursue your first passion.

CONSIDER THIS:

"You don't think on stage. You feel. You just get up there and you're in your own little zone, you know? You know why? Eh? Because we love what we do."

—Keith Richards, lead guitarist of The Rolling Stones

YOUR CHAMPION'S MARGIN TAKEAWAY(S):

_____

_____

_____

_____

_____

_____

_____

_____

CHAPTER 3:

This is Your Career

"Often people attempt to live their lives backwards: they try to have more things, or more money, in order to do more of what they want so that they will be happier. The way it actually works is the reverse. You must first be who you really are, then, do what you need to do, in order to have what you want."

—MARGARET YOUNG

Before you get too far in defining your career interests and plans, ask yourself this question: What are my talents and whose path am I on?

It's up to you to decide whose path you are on. Don't fall into a path or follow a path just because someone else is telling you to do so. Getting input and advice from people you respect and trust is one thing. However, allowing others to define your career can send you in a direction that lands you at a college that doesn't match your needs, where you may study something that doesn't interest you, perhaps interview for jobs you don't want on a career path that doesn't meet your personal needs.

Take a moment to think about whether or not you are following your passion currently or if you actually enjoy what you are doing. Whether you are a student pursuing an internship or full-time job, ask yourself if it's what you want to be doing, where you want to be focused and the direction in which you want to head.

Ask yourself these questions:

1. Whose path am I on?
2. Is this something I want?
3. Is this something I'm passionate about?
4. If I could do *anything* with my time and career, what would it be?

If the answers to these questions—truly honest answers that we demand from you throughout this book—don't align, it's time to reevaluate.

Parents can play an incredibly influential role in our decisions about the things we like and do, as well as the jobs we end up taking. A woman we know graduated from college with a degree in biology. Outside of class, she was a dancer and an artist who dreamed of becoming a fashion designer. However, she earned a degree in biology to make her father happy, she later explained. Her father, a successful corporate lawyer and a brilliant man with high expectations of his children, told her that she needed to major in something useful that would help her get a job after college. The sciences fit that criterion.

Now, you might think we would be in support of practical advice like that, and we are, insofar as it aligns with your passions. As ESPN's former CEO George Bodenheimer says, "Hire people with passion; they will always over deliver." However, without passionate buy-in from you, this runs in direct contradiction to the message we're trying to send, which is to follow your passions, skills and interests in order to pursue a career that aligns with who you are. Employers want and need you to be passionate about your work and your chosen profession. A highly engaged work force can lead a company to success. The long-term reality is much more difficult and less fulfilling for people who are either forced or who force themselves to follow another person's path.

Amid all of your thoughts and reflection on your talents, passions and direction, it is important to think independently about who you want to be and what you actually want to do with your life. How do you want to be known? What values and beliefs are most important to you? What would you do if you had no criteria constraining your pursuit? What would you do if nobody were expecting anything from you? Where would you go if you could blaze your own trail? What if you felt no pressure from your parents, community or lineage? What decisions would you make?

The woman from our previous example ended up working in a nondescript job for two years after college before quitting, pursuing a graduate degree in graphic design, and starting her own firm. She has done work for Deloitte, Calvin Klein and other large-scale entities, and is following her passion to see the world creatively rather than strictly analytically. She chose to break from her father's intended path and, as a result, she is in a much better and fulfilling position for herself.

Taking calculated risks and making independent, informed decisions to pursue your passions is where personalized career management takes root. It's as Abraham Lincoln instructed, "Always bear in mind that your own resolution to success is more important than any other one thing." Think about who you aspire to become and what you want to pursue...then act with tenacity.

YOUR CHAMPION'S MARGIN TAKEAWAY(S):

_____

_____

_____

_____

_____

_____

_____

_____

CHAPTER 4:

Launch Your Career Search

"If you know what you want, you are more apt to recognize it when you see it."

—S. B. FULLER

Now THAT YOU HAVE IDENTIFIED your fundamental talents, passions and interests, you are ready to turn your sights outward to external variables. You are ready to take action on the job-search process itself. However, you may have a fairly broad, and perhaps overwhelming, list as a result of your reflection on favorite classes, extra-curricular activities, natural strengths and career/passion brainstorming. You may be asking yourself, "What am I supposed to do with this?"

As with any decision in business or life, you must account for certain criteria. In business, the criteria are usually led by concerns for resources like money, time and sheer capacity. Each criterion limits the range of solutions and allows you to get closer to the best outcome.

The list of external variables we offer below is robust enough to constrain your analysis. This exercise is meant to help you narrow down your career paths.

Criterion #1: Alignment with Career Interests

Talk with colleagues, professors, alumni and supervisors. Search online to begin to identify careers that relate to your passions and align with your career interests. Talk with friends, family and alumni to better understand and refine your interests and post-college career pursuits. Push yourself beyond simply taking a job to the point where you make conscious moves that will launch your career in exceptional ways.

You may have a passion for the retail industry or you may love working with youth. You may enjoy healthcare, but what does that mean? In what setting do you see yourself? What roles and populations interest you most, and under what circumstances?

This is not meant to be an academic exercise, but rather one to help you more finely tune your search so that you will be able to clear the next set of hurdles.

Take the necessary time to think about whether or not this imagined job aligns with your passions, leverages your strengths and moves you toward your career aspirations.

Criterion #2: Stepping Stone or Ladder

There are companies whose human capital strategy—the way they approach the recruitment, retention and development of human resources—employs an "end-to-end" approach in which they grow their own talent. Others look to recruit top talent from other companies.

Joining a company's trainee program may fit you well, offering you experience in several areas of the business and across most major functional areas. While this approach may appeal to many people, there are an equal number of individuals who are looking to accept a specific role in a range of possible companies. Either choice is fine. Your decision will help you refine your search.

Criterion #3: Geography

Geography matters a lot to some people and not at all to others. If you are intent upon a location, let that be one point of influence in your search. In fact, if this criterion gives you solid grounding in your life, it could be a wonderfully positive influence on your quality of life, your general outlook on life, and as a result, your engagement and productivity at work.

Geography can be a hidden liability in your search and decision-making processes. Many people prematurely and unnecessarily limit their searches to specific geographical regions, and limit their opportunities as a result. We are not recommending that you perform an entirely unconstrained search, but we do recommend allowing yourself a bit of breathing room when while taking your first step in proactive career management.

Trying to manage too many criteria is extremely challenging, so to unfairly burden yourself with the weighty obligation of staying in your hometown or home state seems unnecessarily narrow. Remember: this is about your priorities. If location truly is a major concern, then you have to be willing to make decisions based on that priority. Just be prepared for potential trade-offs as you progress. Trade-offs are personal and relate to your priorities and goals.

Criterion #4: Compensation

An ongoing theme in this book is the challenge to "be honest with yourself." Compensation is a perfect example of why or how that might be more difficult than you think. The issue of compensation is often uncomfortable for a new college graduate, who rarely enters the offer process with information and knowledge. Questions to ask are:

1. What should the offer range be?
2. How much do I need to make (including rent, school loans, car payment and so on)?
3. If, when and how do I negotiate?

Many of us have a dread fascination with it: *How much does he make? How much does she make? Did you hear what so-and-so got offered?! I can't believe he got a signing bonus!* Inevitably, this leads back to what *you* make…which, for some reason, is never quite enough. We find ourselves feeling as if we are not making what we think we ought to, being jealous of what other people make and feeling sheepish or embarrassed about our own desire to make more. If you can say to yourself that compensation is a top priority or that compensation is not a top priority, then you can apply that criterion to your decision and move on.

There are certain career paths that almost guarantee top-tier compensation and some career paths at the other end of the spectrum. How do you determine what priority compensation holds for you?

First, do some basic research to find your profession's expected salary range. This could involve making a list that outlines your expectations for an ideal compensation outcome and then finding a career area that meets your requirement, or drafting a monthly budget to identify your required take-home pay. Second, pick your target to establish a minimum and an ideal pay range. Third, move on to the next step of ensuring you can find something that enriches you personally. However, you must also consider this: What if you can't make a living doing what you love to do?

To understand a market rate and cost of living comparison for your income range, use a cost of living index, which can be found through an Internet search. Most cost of living indices or calculators will use 100 percent as a normalized cost of living and provide city information as a percentage. For instance, a cost of living index reveals that Nashville is approximately 90 percent while New York City is above 140 percent.

The cost of living index gives you a frame of reference to compare salaries across geographies.

Criterion #5: Passions

Henry David Thoreau said, "Pursue a path, however crooked and narrow, in which you can walk with love and reverence." As we noted in Chapter 3, people who follow their passions tend to meet with success and, ultimately, happiness.

Paul offers an example of success in determining natural strengths, interests and passions to create a fulfilling career. He founded and currently leads a highly successful healthcare executive search firm. Paul is excited to go to work every day. His natural inclination to connect with people, to analyze and solve problems, to assist companies in achieving growth plans, to make social and professional connections for others and to boldly ask questions and push for clarity, all align with his chosen career path. He is able to exercise his personal and professional strengths and passions, all while achieving business success.

Ethan is passionate about developing the people around him and empowering them to achieve. For a long time that meant teaching in a classroom and leading within a traditional educational environment. After graduate school and a great deal of reflection, Ethan was able to see a broader application for his passion and skill. He has since found incredible personal, professional and intellectual satisfaction by applying his natural strengths and interests to an emerging business setting. Ethan and Paul have both aligned their talents, passions and interests in their careers.

However, what if your passion doesn't provide a clear opportunity? What if your idea is not currently in the market? What if you think there is a better way to do something? What if you don't want to wait until graduation to really get involved in your chosen profession?

If you are pondering these kinds of questions, we believe you should start, build and run something that offers you the opportunity you seek. However, be sure that your ideas will translate into income. If people will not pay for what you provide, you don't have a business. Some of the business world's greatest success stories have come from people who were fascinated with a small slice of the world. They all started by taking action—so get started!

Given today's amazing access to technology and the accessibility of relationships that technology affords us all, you can create your dream job in a dorm room, garage or anywhere. However, it takes exceptional effort, focus, discipline and sacrifice.

If your passion for a topic, product or service is so strong that you can't deny it, and if the job you envision simply doesn't exist, perhaps you can find an income-producing avenue by creating your own opportunity. You might find a position within a company that offers a step in the right direction. Simultaneously, you may decide that you have a passion, need or opportunity to start a company in parallel. Go for it. Take a pioneering leap in a new direction. The best job may be the one that you create.

CAREER MANAGEMENT: BUILDING NETWORKS

If you are to proactively manage your career from the start, regardless of whether you are about to graduate, whether or not you choose to start your own entrepreneurial venture, you will need to know how to build and utilize your networks. Networking with alumni is something that many colleges tacitly offer, but don't directly teach. Somehow, it falls on the individual to develop these skills.

Alumni are a large and generally approachable group for you to target. Alumni want to help students, and they want to help each other. It's good for a school's reputation to have engaged and gainfully employed alumni. It's good for development and fundraising to have a well-placed and thriving alumni base. It's good for business to have high-quality professional partnerships and resources. Alumni networking can accomplish all of these things, so let's talk about how to access and connect with this group.

CAREER MANAGEMENT CENTER NETWORKING

Your career management center (CMC) counselor should help you identify potential alumni contacts. Ask your CMC counselor to help you connect with alumni who have experience doing what you want to do, or with alumni who share your major and would be willing to discuss possible career paths. The CMC is interested in knowing centers of influence in the alumni network, as well as specific individuals who are either doing what you want to be doing or people who have done what you want to be doing. It only takes a few alumni contacts to help you begin to build your future.

1. **Take Action**: Identify the people, companies and industries that match your strengths, interests, experience and personality to develop a target list. Start from your ideal and expand from there.

2. **Make Contact**: Be prepared. Then be brief, be bright and be gone.

3. **Build Rapport**: Networking is about making personal connections. Alumni and college networks are interested in your pursuits and are willing to provide advice and accept you due to the university connection. You already have mutual interests and a mutual investment. Rapport, then, is up to you. Be yourself.

4. **Establish Timelines:** Set up a weekly or bi-weekly schedule for yourself of tasks to complete on time.

Alumni networks are available through a number of access points. They are relatively risk-free resources, as alumni are often willing to help motivated and well-presented college students. Additionally, fraternities and sororities have networks that expand even beyond the boundaries of your school. Varsity sports teams offer dependable alumni networks. Colleges within a university, graduate schools, honor societies and even special interest clubs offer opportunities to meet professionals. The lesson here is: Leave no stone unturned.

You can look to your career management center, certainly, but be sure to ask about contacts at any of our aforementioned alumni sources. This is a great way to link in with employers who share your passions, alumni who have connections aligned with your interests and people who are predisposed to understand and appreciate your strengths.

The key is to take action. Make a list of the groups to which you belong and talk with each group's leader to find out what he knows about alumni who are connected to the group. Search a database, ask the career center, or contact your school's alumni relations office.

Also, don't forget contacts from an internship or current job supervisors. Tell them you are looking to get in touch with alumni who were involved in a specific group, activity, team or organization. Again, this is about finding common ground with people who can help you leverage the skills you've developed by exploring your interests and passions for, say, debate or computer programming.

Once you get contact names, make a plan for your contact so you can make good use of everyone's time.

The majority of alumni are willing to help you. It is your responsibility to make it easy for them to help you. In an email or phone call, explain who you are, how you got his phone number or email address, the common ground you share and the type of help you're looking for. This frames your expectations and lets your alumni resources know what they can expect, as well.

Obviously, not all alumni contact happens over the phone or email. There are often great opportunities to mix with engaged alumni around campus, at events or at reunions. Take time to reach out to meet new people, and be prepared to speak simply, directly and efficiently about what interests you, what you're looking to do next and what you're interested in long-term. This offers a sort of "past, present and future" for your new advocates and will help them think about ways to help you. It's even worth your time to get business cards with your name and contact information on them so you can leave something as a reminder.

You may wonder if you need to buy coffee or a meal for the people you contact. The answer is no. In fact, you do not need to personally meet with each alumnus. For one, this may not be practical based on your location and the alum's geography, as well as the alumnus' schedule and amount of time he is traveling. Additionally, the alumnus does not need and probably doesn't have the 1-hour-plus commitment it requires to leave his or her house or office, drive to meet you, have coffee or a meal and then drive back. Aside from the fact that most college students and impending or recent graduates do not have the financial capacity to buy meals and coffees in bulk, you also don't need that much time. If you are invited to meet in their office, go when you can. Otherwise a phone call is great. Be practical and realize that phone calls can be very effective, timely and successful. While we do believe that an in-person meeting is better than a phone call, let's be realistic and go with what we can get and then be well prepared, thoughtful and succinct in our pursuit and conversation.

OTHER RESOURCES ON CAMPUS

There are business contacts everywhere you look on a college campus. With a little investigation you can have access to numerous resources, including visiting lecturers, campus career fairs, professors and local businesses in need of students to help with research projects, business plan development and other meaningful projects.

Professors can be good sources for contacts, ideas and advice. Many professors have experience in the business or entrepreneurial community. Ask questions, share your interests and your passions and ask for input based on their experience and what they know about you. Ask something like, "What opportunities do you see that someone in my situation should be learning about or pursuing?" or "If you were in college today, what would you be looking to do after graduation?"

When you go to someone for guidance, be sure to frame your questions to elicit the most useful information. Questions that work include: "What advice would you offer me?" or "What experience(s) would you encourage me to have or pursue related to my career pursuit(s)?"

Students who are your senior or professionals with experience are other important resources when you know how to ask the right questions and develop the right relationships. These types of contacts offer low-cost, low-risk opportunities to gain insight and experience that can be applied to your own search and approach to future work opportunities.

Reach out to peers who have experience in a specific area— perhaps someone you just finished an internship with at one of your target companies or someone who has advanced to the next level of a career path you admire.

Start by asking questions about the sorts of tasks they complete on a regular basis. What are the challenges of their jobs or the best and worst parts of their experiences as interns or employees? Any question that can contribute to or benefit your career pursuit is worth asking.

It takes discipline and a certain measure of humility to be willing to ask for help. However, you won't regret taking the time to seek out these conversations and connection points. They can represent the difference between landing your opportunity and missing out.

LESSONS TO LIVE BY

Time Management:

We believe the college experience is defined by deep engagement in the campus life, thorough investment in your studies, meaningful relationships with your peers and professors and an extracurricular life of service and leadership. Naturally, then, time management is a real-world skill that you can develop in the low-risk environment of college before you enter "the real world." Let's face it: for many people college is the first time they experience autonomy with their schedule and commitments.

Many well-meaning parents have told their children, "College is the one time in life when you don't have a care in the world." Here's the problem: Because of the many distractions and competing priorities, it is not uncommon for the college years to have seemingly vanished by the time you pick up this book. Now is the time to recalibrate your expectations and to develop a disciplined approach to your commitments and your overall consistency of follow-through and performance. Even small sacrifices in the name of organization, discipline and focus will pay huge dividends—even before you graduate.

Here is a list of good habits to practice to make sure that you can apply the appropriate time management skills to internships, and that you will successfully make the transition to full-time employment smoothly after graduation. These lessons and habits are applicable during and after your college experience, so they are worth a second and third consideration.

Time Management Checklist:

❑ Use a daily organizer and keep it with you all the time.

❑ Keep all commitments, appointments, work sessions, workouts, team meetings and personal obligations in your organizer.

❑ Use your daily organizer to invite people to meetings.

❑ Arrive for appointments, meetings and obligations at least five minutes early. If you're early, you're on time; if you're on time, you're late.

❑ When meeting at a new and unknown location, take a "dry run" beforehand to ensure you know how to get there, how long it will take and where to park, if necessary.

❑ Enter homework/study time as a separate appointment and hold yourself to it.

❑ Set an alarm and stick to it.

❑ Do not skip a meeting or gathering if you are expected to attend. If you are running late or must cancel, give others a timely notice and the real reason for your cancellation.

Personal time management takes a fair amount of practice. However, this habit will build your credibility at school and when you join an office for your first internship or job.

YOUR CHAMPION'S MARGIN TAKEAWAY(S):

_____

_____

_____

_____

_____

_____

_____

_____

CHAPTER 5:

The Power
of Goals

"Take a chance! All life is a chance. The man who goes
farthest is generally the one who is willing to do and
dare. The sure-thing boat never gets far from shore."

—DALE CARNEGIE

We WERE BOTH FORTUNATE to have people around us who pushed us to think about our aspirations for the future. They never pushed us to set their goals or told us what goals to set; they simply encouraged us to think about what we wanted to do and to put a plan in place to realize that vision.

At the time, planning for a career seemed like a large and unwieldy task, and it really does force you to slow down and assess who you are, your desires, what you have accomplished and what you really want to be doing. Today, 16 years after college, Paul can tell you that goal setting has been critical to both his business and personal life. The best way to set goals is to simply get started. As with most things that involve solidifying the intangible, that first action here is crucial.

To get started, allow the process to flow freely without editing. Take out a pen and paper or use your computer to brainstorm a list of the things you would like to do. Begin with a simple category, such as your first job out of college. Your goal may involve one of the following: to earn an interview with a specific company or learn how to research an industry; to speak with a certain number of alumni in your chosen industry or functional role; to feel confident talking with business professionals; to set a meeting with someone in your career management center; to interview with your targeted employer(s); to determine where you want to live, to receive and accept an offer; or to decide what you can do and want to do with your degree.

Once you have brainstormed, determine what actions are needed to achieve your goals. Breaking down your goals allows you to see the steps necessary to achieve those goals. For example, once you land a job, perhaps your goal is to become the top sales-person or to expand your computer programming knowledge or lead a marketing project. Write it all down. If you fail to write it down, you allow yourself too much wiggle room and run the risk of deferring a dream and missing out on a potentially rich path.

Articulated goals force you to identify and prioritize what is important to you. Some goals will lie beyond your reach and others will lose their luster as time passes. Conversely, some goals become simple to obtain and some actually grow in intrigue or importance over time. This is normal.

Empower yourself to develop goals that fall into the Big Hairy Audacious Goal (BHAG) category, a concept introduced in 1996 by leadership and management experts Jim Collins and Jerry Porras in an article entitled "Building Your Company's Vision." Your BHAG list will be a collection of challenges that appear huge, looming and nearly unattainable.

Collins and Porras explain: "A true BHAG is clear and compelling, serves as a unifying focal point of effort, and acts as a clear catalyst for team spirit. It has a clear finish line, so the organization can know when it has achieved the goal; people like to shoot for finish lines."

An example of a BHAG may be your desire to become a vice president in your company before you turn 30 or to become the first person in your new-hire class to earn a promotion. Maybe you want to achieve a sales target or an operational performance level usually obtained by those people with four to five years more experience than you have.

Think about BHAGs this way: If you could do anything you wanted in this new role, what would that be? Write down your answers and then create a plan to take action toward your goals. Stretch yourself, set up expectations and scenarios that will allow you to approach or reveal your true potential.

––––––––––––

Just by picking up this book you have indicated that you are driven to achieve something significant, so we can also assume you have a great deal of capacity to make things happen. As a high achiever, your collection of goals is likely to contain a long list of action points and steps to guide you toward the milestones you intend to reach. From this, you will probably identify 5 to 10 goals you want to achieve in the next year. While it is tempting to create a long list, you run the risk of stretching yourself too thin, diluting the results and missing out on your true capacity for rich achievement.

We want you to have a manageable number of goals in order to ramp up your effectiveness. Our experience suggests that a list of three to five goals is manageable without being overwhelming. Burn Your Resume aims to expose you to the concept of goal setting and engage you in setting lofty goals from the beginning of your career through your first years of employment. In your new role, in your new environment, you will need the right goals and you will need habit and repetition as you move through you career.

PLANNING FOR SUCCESS:

So far, we have talked about setting goals specific to your first job out of college. We encourage you to organize your annual goals in the following six categories. Try to limit each category to one to two items so no one goal dominates all of your time, and the overall list won't overwhelm you.

Listed alphabetically, try using the following categories for goal setting:

1. **Career:** What do you want to start, finish, prepare for or accomplish in the coming year?
2. **Community:** What organization(s) do you want to continue to support or begin involvement with during the coming year?

3. **Faith:** Have you defined your character? Are you interested in thinking about or developing your faith, becoming involved in a local place of worship, or increasing your commitment?

4. **Finances:** Do you want to save for a future event, trip, purchase or need? Do you want to earn a certain income, which is probably easier to do if you have a high percentage of variable income opportunity? Do you want to pay off a debt or avoid debt altogether?

5. **Personal:** Do you want to start or continue a healthy lifestyle of exercise, diet, rest and overall personal well-being? Do you have a purchase or investment you are interested in making? Is there a skill you want to learn or further develop? Is there a relationship you need or want to work on?

6. **Relationships:** Do you want to develop a relationship or end a bad relationship? Do you want to spend more time with family members? Do you want to expand your friendships and/or build stronger friendships with those you've already established?

By taking the time to reflect on your true desires, the range of your capacity and the steps that need to happen in order to achieve your vision of the future, you are planning for your future success. Once you've made your plan, get to work and achieve it.

YOUR CHAMPION'S MARGIN TAKEAWAY(S):

_____

_____

_____

_____

_____

_____

_____

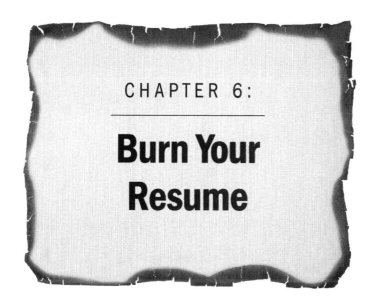

CHAPTER 6:

Burn Your Resume

"Most people who graduate from college think they have to make a perfect choice. Is it Goldman Sachs? Is it Google? Is it Apple? They think that their first job is going to determine their career, if not their life. Looking back, that's absolutely incorrect."

—GUY KAWASAKI

YOU MAY BE WONDERING why there is a chapter about crafting a resume in a book entitled *Burn Your Resume*. The book's title is a bold statement about the changing rules in the job-search process: the old rules no longer apply.

We are not interested in doing away with your resume. We are interested, however, in doing away with your reliance on it. We want you to control the message it broadcasts. We want you to make proactive and informed decisions that target your goals and drive your purpose. Ultimately, an exceptional resume is a tool to help unlock that first-round interview invitation. So spend time breaking down your resume into its essential pieces and then restructure it to tell your story, rather than allowing it to determine your path.

Given that there are already thousands of books on Amazon.com that provide outlines and guidelines for your resume, our goal is to teach you content over style. In this chapter you will find the main sections of a resume organized in a way that will help you best communicate the key information your reader needs to understand.

Again, this is a how-to perspective that will enable you to separate yourself from the competition.

WHAT SHOULD YOUR RESUME COMMUNICATE?

Perhaps you are familiar with the "Elevator Pitch," which is the amount of time you have to share your prime qualities, desired role and key objectives if you were to unexpectedly find yourself traveling between floors in an elevator with a hiring manager.

Take time right now to measure 30 seconds just so you can see what it feels like. In reviewing your resume, be aware that the same 30-second window represents the amount of time a hiring manager will take to scan your resume as he works through a stack to set up first-round interviews. The most important purpose of your resume is to communicate a clear direction and content flow in a very short timeframe. If you know how to frame and discuss your experiences and successes, you will have no problem crafting a resume that gets you noticed.

Now you know exactly how narrow your window of opportunity is. Because of this criterion, we want you to drive your resume construction toward the following fundamentals: your resume needs to be *Clear, Concise, Consistent* and *Connected*. Determine the message you want to convey and the image you want to portray and make sure it is at least relevant to the demands of the job description. Be sure it tells a meaningful story and that it piques the interest of the person who reviews it by answering the question, "Why would I want to talk with you?"

Again, you should expect that the typical hiring manager or recruiter will not spend more than 30 seconds scanning your resume. Therefore, build your resume with the intention of getting yourself noticed.

To get started, brainstorm and write down everything you have done in three sections: Education, Experience and Community. Go in chronological order and start writing the experiences you have had, without a filter. Once finished, it's time to shape your resume to be clear, concise, consistent and connected.

Clear:

Remember that you have only 30 seconds to make the reviewer want to talk with you, so be sure that your message is clear. Your reviewer should be saying, "I can see that he wants to talk to me about this role and I can see why he is interested in this position and/or company. I want to know more." Make sure your information demonstrates continuity of thought, intent and action.

Concise:

Be brief but illustrative in your writing. There is no need to fill space. Tell the reviewer what he or she needs to know. "Situation,

Task, Action, Result" (STAR) or "Situation, Action, Outcome" (SAO) is the structure you should use when telling your story in resume form. This means you help the reader understand what the situation was, what you did to impact the situation or resolve the issue and the outcome of your intervention. Expressing your experience as a story allows people to understand and translate your experience into their business.

Break your work down using action words (verbs that communicate progress and influence) and distill your impact down to its core. Rather than soft, flowery, conversational language, consider using some of the following words as lead-ins to your bullet points: led, drove, spearheaded, managed, oversaw, integrated, analyzed, resolved, proposed, developed, launched, or created. Find the tone that is right for you.

Be crisp and to-the-point with your bullets and don't be afraid to present data as data. Be sure to include the things you did that yielded positive results. However, take the time to revise your explanations until they are bare-bones, core, fundamental descriptions of the point you're making.

Consistent:

Consistency is another key in telling a compelling story in less than 30 seconds. What does this mean? Well, if your resume has gaps, holes or vague language that makes the reviewer question its truth, then you're already at risk of ending up in the rejection pile. Did you work at a community center and then intern at a tech firm and then do an independent study about nursing home management? If so, how do you think that reads on your resume? What do you think that tells your reviewer? If it's your resume and you don't know, how can you expect the reviewer to know?

It is your responsibility to find and highlight common threads between seemingly disparate features on your resume. Highlight them with common language and a common emphasis on results. This will help convince a reviewer that you can draw lessons from experience, apply them to new settings and continue to develop your ability to impact a situation.

Connected:

When competing for a job opportunity, experience and results are golden. Results are what hiring managers are looking for. They want to see that you can influence a situation and achieve positive results or work through a challenging environment or outcome. However, if your experience occurs across a range of roles, industries or disciplines, you may find it difficult to have your resume tell a concise story. You need to have a clear story to connect with your reviewer's perspective and satisfy them. Your ability to tell a clear and concise story is critical.

Ethan encountered challenges with his resume at the start of his job search process. While he had graduated with high honors, worked a number of internships and risen to a leadership position in his jobs, he struggled to land first-round interviews. The problem: he hadn't clearly articulated his experience with his job pursuits.

The lessons Ethan learned are shared with you throughout this chapter. He thought his resume told this story: "Here's a guy who has excelled in every environment and will excel in yours." However, it's more likely that the reviewer looked at his resume, paused at "Harvard," and then moved on to the section about his experience, which is where the message may have gotten less clear or obvious. Ethan's resume was a series of stand-alone accomplishments rather than a cohesive story.

After working with Paul to supercharge his search, Ethan began to think about how to present his accomplishments from the hiring manager's perspective. Almost immediately after revising his resume and talking points, he began interviewing and ultimately received two excellent offers that aligned his passions, interests and skills.

The ability to connect with your audience depends on how you choose to write bullets, feature your accomplishments and present yourself on paper. You have to tell the story of what you have done and what you want to do with a clear message so the reader is able to visualize how you could benefit his company. Without the ability to connect, the manager cannot be expected to want to know more about you.

You make yourself "connectable" by using language familiar

to the reviewer, language that is featured in the job description and indicates your knowledge of the role's challenges and by deliberately communicating who you are in a clear and compelling story.

Structure is a big part of the challenge. When you start editing, follow these guidelines to help shape the message and create your image:

- **Say what you've done.** Be open and clear about your achievements and direction.
- **Stay concise, focused and aligned.** Everything should aim to your job/career goal.
- **Relate points to your target.** Achievements, involvement and experience should tie together.
- **Show interest.** What are you doing to show the employer you are serious about what you're talking about?

HOW TO BUILD A WINNING RESUME

There is a structure to successful resume-building. In fact, many of you who have picked up this book are attending schools with resume templates. If your career center has a preferred resume style, feel free to use it. They may have developed it for continuity within the university's system and database. You can pick your style; we want to help with the substance. We will provide a resume template that provides the meaningful content and detail you need to include, because remember: you only have 30 seconds to make an impact, so your information needs to be organized.

Section: **HEADER**

First and Last name

(*Okay for this font to be larger than your contact information*)

Email address and cell phone number

City, State and Zip Code

(*The reader will assume this address to be your current or permanent address. If you have two addresses, it's okay to list both.*)

Make sure you choose a crisp, professional font for your resume, slightly larger than the body of your resume. We prefer Times New Roman. You want your reviewer to have easy access to your content and to be able to make sense of information, and you want to make your name familiar.

Section: **EDUCATION**

EDUCATION

ABC College or University

Expected date of Graduation

Degree & current year (freshman, sophomore, junior or senior)

Major and GPA (Major GPA and Overall GPA)

Honors or Achievements, Additional Coursework or Training, Languages and Summer Studies Abroad

The first section of your winning resume is Education. Above all, be sure to follow this advice from Paul: "Tell me you're smart and that you applied yourself in school." Show your reviewer that you were able to balance classroom responsibilities with real-world responsibilities. Emphasize your leadership, achievements and self-sufficiency, especially if they are strengths of yours.

List the information about your education, beginning with your most recent (or impending) accomplishment first. Be sure to include the name and location of your university, as well as your course of study and any other exceptional accomplishments that contribute to your cohesive and connectable story. In case you are wondering, you need to include your GPA.

> *Section:* **EXPERIENCE**
> EXPERIENCE
> **Company:** Give a one-sentence description if it's not a commonly recognized company or if you need to describe the unit you worked in within a larger organization.
> **Title:** Intern, Summer Associate, Marketing Associate, Assistant to the Vice President, etc.
> **Location and Dates:** Where and when did you work?

Tell the reader what you are doing to pursue career interests. This can include paid and unpaid work, community volunteer opportunities, internships and so on. By the time you graduate college you will probably have two to three different experiences to discuss. With each company or organization, you will use one to three bullet points to highlight your experience. Detail these bullet points in terms of your specific role and performance accomplishment or contribution you provided.

Plan to fit your entire resume on one page. If your text runs onto a second page, condense bullet points or eliminate experiences less relevant or recent to your career pursuits. For instance, you may have been a lifeguard between your freshman and sophomore years, which is a fine summer job. However, if you also have internships and summer jobs with companies in your desired field, you should cut the lifeguarding job to keep your resume to the appropriate length.

Here are a few examples of "STAR" or "SAO" structured bullets:

1. Helped to organize, plan and promote an annual race, including recruiting sponsors and organizing race-day activities. Race included 500 participants and raised $10,000 for (*describe here*).
2. Researched and co-wrote a business plan to (*describe here*). Since writing the plan, we have started operating the business and have generated $25,000 in total revenue.

3. Hired as campus summer sales representative or hired campus summer sales representatives at (*number*) colleges and generated (*dollar amount*) in revenue.

4. Wrote a computer program in Perl, Basic, JAVA or .net, to automate (*describe here*).

5. Conducted industry financial analysis to understand financial returns from publicly traded companies and developed model for Company's growth projections.

6. Waited tables, Cooked or Managed a restaurant's evening shift with 10 employees and served (*number*) meals daily or during your shift.

7. Started and developed yard / pool maintenance business. Grew business to serve 30 summer clients, generating $5,000 in total summer/annual revenue.

8. Summer intern or associate in law firm/accounting firm/ consulting firm supporting manager in research, file organization and case preparation for clients in the following sectors: Healthcare, Technology and Manufacturing.

9. Traveled for one month to rural parts of the world to provide HIV education to young people from a small village. The goal was to improve healthy lifestyles in the developing area.

10. Worked full-time while attending college and throughout summers in the family business. (*Provide definition of the business and your role.*)

Remember to show the reader that you're experienced and interested in what you're pursuing. This gets back to the point about being consistent. You have to be able to indicate that your experience sets you up for an understandable and obvious "next step" in this role.

Show the reviewer how you've become involved in your chosen areas of interest. Include all of your experiences so you can gain some perspective on it before you edit down the list. Be sure to include paid, unpaid, volunteer and intern experience. Make sure the details align with your goal and with the clear, consistent message of your resume.

Did your featured interest get sparked by an internship, from a high school experience, from a summer job, or a work-study program? Was it a specific class that led you to study or research in a certain area that blossomed into part-time work with a local sports team, for example? What does all of this tell you about yourself? These are important questions to ask in order to understand the reviewer's perspective.

Highlight the fact that your experience aligns with your achievements and the job you're pursuing. Experience will reassure the reviewer that you have exposure to a professional or semi-professional environment and that you know how to move effectively through that environment. When you underscore these points with actions taken that resulted in achievements, you're well on your way to having a memorable resume.

> *Section:* **COMMUNITY**
>
> **COMMUNITY:**
>
> **Organization:** state your role and tenure
>
> Columnist or editor for school paper;
>
> Leadership role in organization: student body, social organization, athletics, etc.
>
> Developed websites for small businesses.
>
> Volunteered at the local children's hospital one day per week reading to children.
>
> Mentored incoming freshmen to assist in high school-to-college transition.

This section should introduce your personal passions and interests. It should tell the reader that you recognize that you can have an impact outside of your personal pursuits. Your involvement in other organizations demonstrates all of this, including professional organizations, companies, athletics, social involvement and volunteering positions.

Companies are increasingly interested in community involvement. Your reviewers will wonder, "Is this person active in the community, trade groups or organizations of interest?" Ask yourself: Where do I spend time? Do I know and show that the world is larger than just me? Am I doing anything to serve something greater than myself?

This is important because it suggests you are a collaborative and invested person who can be counted on to work hard for things you believe in. It tells employers that you are at least worth a second look because you have a value system and are willing to take action and initiative without direct instruction. Highlight this involvement in your Community section by listing the organizations, the roles you've played and the results of your involvement. Similarly, you can feature personal awards, accomplishments and certifications. Do you speak any other languages? Do you have any outstanding details that don't fit elsewhere in the story of your resume? If that's the case, make sure that it adds to, rather than detracts from, the value of your candidacy.

Try to think about your resume from your reviewer's perspective. What would it take for you to invest in the "you" represented on your resume? Then fill the gaps and fix the problems, and you will see a change in the way people respond to your candidacy. This holds true for honors and activities, software skills and professional certifications, offices held, clubs or sports played and even creative professional activities. Make sure that it demonstrates your ability to communicate and interact with people, to lead and influence groups, to affect positive outcomes and to drive for achievements.

If you want to feature your involvement in a fraternity or sorority, be sure that the title, responsibilities and impact of your leadership are worthy of the story you're telling throughout your resume. Ultimately, you want to make sure that your resume strikes a balance, maintains a balance and communicates that balance.

Section: **REFERENCES**

REFERENCES: List Name, Current Role, Phone Number and Context for your relationship

Many young people try to include a list of personal and professional references in the body of their resume. We think this runs the risk of undercutting your credibility as a viable and low-risk investment because it can be misinterpreted in ways that are outside your control.

Remember, your resume should be a clear, concise, consistent, connected message. Therefore, we recommend that if you are compelled or required to include references, create a separate document that is specifically intended to feature the names, contact information and relevant details about these people. This way, you aren't implying that these individuals are proxies for your experience, which could be inferred from having them at the bottom of your resume. Rather, you are simply offering your reviewer another perspective on you, the candidate, as a professional.

As long as you have contemplated the message you want to convey and the identity you want to maintain, and as long as your references will reinforce the momentum you have created, then you should feel free to include your references, if you think it necessary or references have been requested.

COVER LETTER

Many career advisors will tell you that recruiters and hiring manages either don't look at cover letters or don't have time to look at them. We have even heard that cover letters can serve as a detriment to an application. Nonetheless, we want to provide a framework for those who want to use cover letters.

A cover letter should be cordial, direct, succinct and candid. Formatting should be similar to a standard business letter regarding date, address, salutation, body text, complimentary close, signature line, cell phone and email address.

The body of a cover letter should be shorter than 10 sentences. Introduce yourself, offer context for your application and for yourself as a candidate, state your experience as it relates to the position and express your interest to talk with the firm or company.

Include a cover letter with your name signed in blue or black if you are submitting a hard copy of resume. If you are submitting electronically, either close with your name typed or use an electronic signature, if you are able.

YOUR CHAMPION'S MARGIN TAKEAWAY(S):

_____

_____

_____

_____

_____

_____

_____

_____

CHAPTER 7

How to
Network

"If people knew how hard I worked to get my mastery,
it wouldn't seem so wonderful after all."

—MICHELANGELO

CAREER EXPERTS EMPHASIZE the importance of networking; however, few of them explain how to network. Where do you go? What do you do? What do you say? What's the first step?

Networking is an important skill that requires practice. Developing a networking ability will assist you in landing internships and your first job out of college, setting up your exceptional career.

It's been said that fewer than 20 percent of the open positions and meaningful employment opportunities that exist are posted online. However, many people still put significant resources into their job search via online job boards. Bad decision. Fighting the masses for a small percentage of the opportunities is not where you want to compete.

Let's define networking. Dictionary.com defines networking as a supportive system of sharing information and services among individuals and groups having a common interest. We want to emphasize the importance of "a supportive system" in restating this as "building personal connections."

You may think networking means jumping on LinkedIn, contacting your Facebook friend list, or blasting your Twitter followers for a lead. The digital route is certainly one to pursue. With push-button worldwide connectivity via technology, you can span vast distances instantaneously and access existing relationships for bank-shot introductions.

However, we believe that proactive, exceptional networking in the 21st century is about finding a common bond with another individual and turning yourself from an unknown to an interesting individual. It's about becoming familiar and decreasing the perceived risk around you as a candidate. It's about building personal connections. Building personal connections. Building personal connections…which means you need a foundation, you need a plan and you need practice.

Personal connection and a measure of familiarity can be a major differentiator and a great way to maintain personal connections through social media, such as LinkedIn and Facebook.

FACEBOOK:

Facebook is a great resource for keeping in touch with people and meeting potential future collaborators, partners and employers. However, Facebook can be a big strike against you if someone finds a picture of you in a compromising state (involving alcohol, drugs, or other unsavory behavior). Be sure that while you're crafting your personal professional brand, you remain aware of the digital trail you've left behind and proactively manage the message that you're communicating.

LINKEDIN:

The power of LinkedIn is that it allows you, as a candidate and a professional, to expand your network with the express intent of getting your name and personal professional brand out into the marketplace of people who can search for you through specific criteria.

Make sure that you create a page that highlights your professional strengths, interests and goals. With a picture, digital resume and a few targeted references, you can ensure that you meet the minimum threshold to represent yourself as a viable, engaged, driven and valuable candidate that a potential employer can find online with ease to help them past any initial hesitation they may have.

OTHERS:

There will continue to be emerging popular social media resources. One example is Google+, which defines itself as a resource that "makes connecting on the Web more like connecting in the real world." Google+ and other social media sites to come will continue to weave in and out of our lives.

Remember that technology can be a quiet enemy. If you're not careful, it can bite you. As a tool for success, make sure that you apply a minimal amount of energy and attention to social media to ensure that you help lend depth and breadth to your candidacy in a way that you control.

The Personal Connection

Networking is about making personal connections. Networking to learn about people, their interests and how you can help them will provide interesting new relationships and positive business outcomes. In order to achieve these things, you have to be relatable, personable and memorable. This takes time, practice and probably a little bit of initial awkwardness to achieve.

Paul is an extrovert, a seasoned and professional veteran networker, but his skills weren't inherent. He had to develop a balanced skill set of boldness, confidence, wit and conversational ability. All of us have work to do in this arena, so take time to determine the message you want to send every time you reach out to shake a hand. It is about personal familiarity, personal trust and personal contacts.

You may be asking yourself why "personal" matters at all, since this is about being professional. Early in his job search process, Ethan asked the same question. At the time, he would tell you that he believed he was living in a meritocracy, where his achievements, performance and consistent success would speak for themselves in his job search. Consider this for a moment, because you may be feeling the same "I can do anything, I just need an opportunity" kind of sentiment. Opportunity is something that requires a certain price of admission. You need to speak the language of your potential network contact and the industry of your choice in order to be invited in. You want to make choosing you or, in this case, learning about and remembering you as easy as possible for the person with whom you are speaking.

Another reason the personal connection is important is because, even as our world becomes more automated, more digital, more remote and more progressive, businesses are still run by people. Call it what you will, but business leaders and hiring managers—many of whom are members of more traditional generations—are hard-wired to require a personal assessment and the establishment of a certain rapport before investing in a business decision. In your case, that business decision is you, the personal assessment is through a meeting and the establishment of rapport depends on your ability to:

- **Know yourself:** Who you are and want to be, and what you want to do.
- **Know your audience:** What they have, what they need and what they like.

- **Know your entrance:** When, where, how and why to introduce yourself.
- **Know your stuff:** What you offer relative to organizational and industry trends.
- **Know your exit:** After engaging with another professional, know when and how to leave.

Utilizing these five points will set you up for success with a networking opportunity. Most career experts will tell you that networking is important and we are here to tell you how to network. But rest assured that networking perfection is not the goal. Vince Lombardi, one of the most revered coaches in the history of the NFL, explained, "Perfection is not attainable, but if we chase perfection we can catch excellence." That is our point.

NETWORKING IN ACTION

Know Yourself:

Start this process by clearly articulating to yourself what you do or are looking to do. If you can't explain it to yourself, you won't be able to explain it to anyone else.

As we had you do in the first sections of this book, take the time to refine your message and distill your points. You can look back at your notes, at the path you laid out for yourself, at the distinguishing factors that define your strengths, passions and professional aspirations and you can then distill your message.

For Paul, it might be, "I've always been passionate about meeting and learning about individuals. I've built my professional life around connecting talented people with exciting companies." For Ethan, it might be, "I'm passionate about the power of education in business, and my professional goal is to optimize organizational performance."

Assume you are looking to network with people who share that interest, have that need, or can help connect you with someone who does. A simple declarative statement such as either of those is a good place to start.

Know the Audience:

At this early stage, it helps to consider your target contact's point of view. What are his concerns? What are his priorities? What are his professional strengths, weaknesses, surpluses and needs? What are his interests and pursuits? What clubs, associations, pastimes, alma maters, or other backgrounds might you have in common? This information provides grist for the conversational mill when you meet, helps you understand how to shape your message and helps puts you at ease during what can often be nerve-wracking initial contact.

Know Your Entrance:

It is important to understand how to make the first in-person introduction. Hovering awkwardly outside a circle is a no-no. Pacing back and forth, hoping to make eye contact and get invited in is a no-no. Barging through a crowd of people is a no-no.

If you are at networking event, ask the host/hostess or a colleague for help in meeting a specific individual. If you are at a breakfast or social event, look for a light break in the conversation, then approach and politely excuse your interruption before explaining why you want to meet.

For example: "I hope you'll excuse me. My name is (*insert name*) and I would like to introduce myself."

If the person you want to meet appears to be in a serious or focused conversation, your best move is to hold and reconsider in 5, 10 or 20 minutes. Your goal is to stay away from extremes: be neither too meek, nor too bold.

Know Your Stuff:

Come prepared to engage a business professional and be sure that you are equipped to handle questions, contribute interesting or worthy points and that you can represent yourself as a motivated professional.

If you plan to meet someone specific, take the time to prepare. If you have the time for a 20-minute research session, refer back to our guide about how to perform industry research. Otherwise, take a moment to compose your thoughts, put yourself in your target's shoes and consider his or her perspective.

Plan your approach and what you want to say. If you simply don't have much time to prepare before meeting someone, or if there will be too many people present to prepare for a specific individual or group of individuals, plan for the points you want to make. You can plan these points well in advance of the meeting and use them as common points to discuss when meeting any professional. Prepare a mental list of some questions you may ask that are general, but good conversation points. Make a mental list of a few germane points to contribute to the conversation, as well.

HOW TO INTRODUCE YOURSELF AND TALK ABOUT YOUR MAJOR, CAREER INTERESTS AND PURSUITS.

I attend (*insert here*) college / university and my major is (*insert here*). I'm graduating in the spring and I will be looking for a role as a (*insert here*) / or in the (*insert here*) industry / or located in (*insert here*). I have interned or worked for (*insert here*) in a role where I was (*insert here*). My career interest is (*insert here*.)

Note: *This statement needs to be tight and succinct. You will lose the attention of your contact if this takes more than a minute to communicate.*)

Know Your Exit:

Being memorable doesn't mean being clingy or dominating another person's time. In a networking situation, be sensitive to the probability that other people want time with your target. Demonstrate that you can meet and have a conversation in a short amount of time and that you can leave the door open to future conversation. That is memorable.

You've found your opening, introduced yourself, had a message, asked good questions, engaged in informed dialogue and expressed an interest in following up. At this point you should exchange cards, thank the individual for his or her time, say that you look forward to being in touch and leave. You will have been effective with your time and will have created an experience that is real, personal and polished.

BE BRIEF, BE BRIGHT AND BE GONE

Business executives do not expect you to have in-depth knowledge equal to their experience. Asking a few thoughtful questions and answering one or two questions in an intelligent manner defines success in a networking event. It's at this point that many people begin to feel comfortable and then want to stand around with the business leader, but don't have anything further to add. This is the time for you to leave. Be brief, be bright and be gone.

This interaction can take 3 to 4 minutes or up to 10 to 15 minutes, depending on the level of engagement you are able to provide based on responses and the body language the contact is giving you. If you sense the conversation is over and you have nothing else to offer, that is a great time to leave. They expect you to be professional, intelligent, socially aware and interesting to the point they look forward to talking further with you.

Leave on a positive note. You can leave with a simple comment that you enjoyed meeting, enjoyed the discussion and would look forward to talking again. You'll probably receive a positive response, which is an indirect path to follow up with this person if or when you have a need or interest to do so.

Be brief, be bright and be gone so that they think, "Hmmm... smart person. Enjoyable." Your contacts probably won't think about it much more than that, but when you do meet again, they will greet you warmly and you'll find the discussion to be much richer, more comfortable and easily re-engaged.

YOUR CHAMPION'S MARGIN TAKEAWAY(S):

_____

_____

_____

_____

CHAPTER 8

Making Contact

"I have never worried about action, but only inaction."

—WINSTON CHURCHILL

YOU ARE MAKING PROGRESS and are now interested in making calls to alumni and professionals associated with your school or university. When you're looking for information, a call is great. When you are looking to be connected with people in an alumnus' area of expertise, a call is great. When you are trying to find out how to get a foot in the door in a specific industry or how to get in touch with a specific person in this individual's network, a call is great. A phone call is an effective way to utilize your network.

We believe in taking action and making the call now. There is no such thing as a perfect time. However, if are going to make calls, we suggest you make time either in the early morning or late afternoon.

Paul has found in business development and recruiting that the best time to catch someone is before her day starts or when the day is winding down. At these times, you'll often find that an assistant is not yet in or has already left for the day so the individual is likely to answer her own phone. However, if you can only make the call during the day, do it then.

While your success rate with cold calls will be low, we are not opposed to the cold call when you don't have another avenue. If you have an email address you may find that you can warm up a call by first emailing the individual and asking for a brief time to talk.

Be prepared. You can make a call or use an email to set up a 10 to 15-minute time to talk. In your email exchange, let your contact know that you have three to five questions you have and show that you appreciate his or her time by suggesting that you only need 10 to 15 minutes of time.

PHONE CALL TEMPLATE:

[Hello _____. My name is (your name) and I was given your name by (contact's name). I am a current student at _____ studying _____. I am calling because I will soon graduate and I'm on a job search. I also have _____ year(s) of experience doing _____. I am most excited / interested to pursue a job in _____ or a role in the _____ industry. May we schedule 10 minutes to talk by phone, so I can hear your thoughts on my job search and discuss possible networking referrals you may think of? (If this is a voice message, clearly articulate your name and phone number, with area code, two times.)

Both of us have had students reach out to us without a plan and those conversations are difficult, time-consuming and non-productive. Do your pre-call work to make sure you know what you're looking to gain, to offer your contact a context and to avoid wasting the time.

To begin to create momentum for yourself, set aside a 30-minute window of time when you can call three to five alumni. You may reach voicemail or the assistant for each of the alumni, which is fine. Leave a succinct and friendly message. Suggest one or two times your contact can call you back or leave a message saying that you will try her back at a specific time. If you provide dates or times for a call, be accountable to those times.

If it's your first voice message, indicate a time you will call her back. Your second attempt should be within one to two days—not one to two hours. Remember that you are a professional trying to reach another professional, so you don't want to come across as desperate. If you don't reach this person on your second attempt, leave your email and phone number and ask if they will let you know a time she can talk for 5 to 10 minutes.

Your voice message should be succinct, personable and professional. If you ask for 5 to 10 minutes, yet your message rambles on and on, the listener will most likely not believe you can have a conversation in 5 to 10 minutes. Perception is reality, and if you want to reach your audience you need to think through your message and your body language, and body language comes through the phone.

If you leave two messages and you don't hear back, you have either contacted someone who is too busy to get back with you or who is not able or interested in helping you.

If you want to make a third and final attempt, wait one week and call for a third and final time. We do not recommend leaving more than three messages or total contacts, and an email is considered a contact.

Let's use this example: You called and left your desired contact a message on a Monday. She didn't respond either because she's busy or she's trying to see how interested you really are in talking with her. You can try her again on Wednesday afternoon or sometime on Thursday. If you don't hear back by the following Tuesday afternoon or Wednesday morning, make a final attempt.

Your last point of contact message or email may be as follows:

"Hello _____, this is (*your name*). I wanted to leave you one final message to see if we might talk for 5 to 10 minutes. I understand you are busy and I can commit to keeping our call to 5 to 10 minutes. If you are willing to set aside a few minutes, please let me know one or two times in the coming week that are good for you to talk. I appreciate it, (*contact's name*). My cell phone number is _____. Again, my cell is _____. Thank you for your time." (Note: it is helpful to state your phone number two times.)

Communicating with Contacts:

If you catch this person on the phone the first time you call, be succinct, professional and personable. Tell him or her why you're calling and ask for 5 to 10 minutes to talk about your job pursuits. Do not assume that when you call and initially connect that you will have caught the person at a good time. So, do not jump right into your job search. You are calling to ask for a brief time to talk about the fact that you're graduating college and you have a few areas of professional interest, one of which is related to the person you are calling.

You should be prepared to set up a time to call her back. However, be prepared for the person to tell you that he has a few minutes right then to talk. If this happens, tell her you want to quickly frame the purpose of your call. Consider writing all of your points down in order to avoid stumbles or unnecessary awkwardness.

Here is a good example of how to begin the conversation:

- Great, thank you for taking the time now.
- My name is _____. (Note: It often takes people hearing your name three times before they will remember your name.)
- I will graduate this spring from _____ with a degree in _____.
- During college I have interned and worked in either (functional role) or (industry / type of business (start-up, small, medium, Fortune, etc.).
- I will soon be graduating and I am interested in pursuing a role as a _____ in the following business _____ and/or _____.

The entire "framing" introduction should take less than 60 seconds. Remember to practice saying this to yourself, your parents, friends, significant other or your personal voicemail before talking with a real-life alumnus and networking resource.

"I appreciate your time and am interested in your perspective on the following" (ideas for you to use are below). Ask one question and stop... don't keep talking:

- Your current role as _____ is a role I can see myself doing in my career. I'm interested to hear your input about how to best get started on that path.
- Your industry is very appealing to me and I would like to start my career in this industry. I would like to hear your thoughts about the best way to enter this industry. Are there companies you suggest that might get me started on a better road than others? (Alternatively, since you have researched the industry as you prepared for this call, you can let the person know that you have a few specific companies in mind and you would like to ask if there are contacts he could refer to you to help in your networking and career pursuit.)
- You are in a geography that interests me (e.g., Nashville, West Coast, international, etc.). I would like to have this type of role and want to hear who you think is well-networked in this geography.

If she asks you to call back, schedule a time and reiterate that you need only 10 minutes to talk. Then put the date, time and contact number into your schedule. It's important that you have your schedule with you so that you can confirm the date, time and number to call.

Be Accountable:

Once the call is set, do not miss it. Alumni are great resources and they are willing to help. However, nothing will cause you to lose credibility more quickly than missing a scheduled call. Few excuses will work since the people you are contacting have also been to college and know the atmosphere. They also know that the business world expects professionalism, and that missing calls and meetings you set is not tolerated. Though exaggerated, it might help you to think about it this way: If you set up a call and then you miss it for a reason other than a grievous accident or your own personal death, do not bother calling back.

The Meeting is Set:

An in-person meeting allows you to visually present yourself as a professional, demonstrate excitement and interest in the conversation, demonstrate that you are prepared for the brief meeting and communicate that you are serious about what you want to do. However, the reality is that you won't always be able to meet in person.

Here are a few things to think about when talking on the phone:

- **Smile when you talk.** It seems awkward to do this, but your smile will come through on the other end of the phone.
- **Stand up or sit up straight.** Again, body language comes through over the phone, as well.
- **Talk in a paced manner and use inflection.** Let your tone express that you have energy, excitement and interest in the conversation, but don't overdo it like you are trying to sell a once-in-a-lifetime opportunity.
- **Keep it brief.** You're on the call to hear the other person's insights and recommendations. Make your point, ask your question and then stop talking and listen. If you feel like the conversation is more than 50/50, with you talking more, you are over-doing it. Early in Paul's career, he was told by his manager to ask a question and then spin the receiver so that the phone's mouthpiece was back below his chin. That caused him to have to move the phone back to his mouth in order to talk, which prevented him from interrupting the other person's flow. It also provided a split-second in the conversation for either the other person to continue with a thought or for him to appear planned and thoughtful in his response or follow-up question.
- **Be aware of time.** You may find yourself exceeding the 10 minutes you requested. That is positive as long as the

other person is engaged and continuing to offer insight. At or before the 10-minute mark, you may realize that you are done with questions, at which time you can thank her and ask for a networking contact. Or you can indicate that you're sensitive to her time and wrap up the call. If the conversation continues, keep your antennas up. Your contact may be thinking about bringing you in to talk in person. They may be part of a company that would hire your profile, so she may be determining whether to bring you in or refer you to a hiring manager. Or she may simply be impressed with you and willing to help a young person like you.

Ask any remaining questions you have and then thank her for the time and perspective. If your contact does not provide you with the name of a specific person, you can either ask for another contact with additional or different perspectives or ask if you can email or call her in a couple days for a referral.

If the individual agrees with being contacted again in a few days, email is fine. Keep your email brief—you do not have to articulate the entire conversation you just had. She will remember you and have an impression of you. Express your appreciation for her time, let her know you have attached your resume, and that you appreciate additional references and networking contacts they will provide.

Exceptional Follow-through: Consistency matters a lot when following up and following through. Following up in a reasonable timeline is noticeable. Doing it consistently is impressive. Wait no more than a day or two from your first meeting to initiate your follow-up. Your timeline will appropriately communicate your interest and commitment to the relationships and the opportunity. Following up with a personal letter is a nice touch and will help you stand out from the competition.

YOUR CHAMPION'S MARGIN TAKEAWAY(S):

_____

_____

_____

_____

_____

_____

_____

_____

CHAPTER 9

Growing Your Network

"I not only use all the brains that I have, but all that I can borrow."

—WOODROW WILSON

WHEN IS THE BEST TIME for you to introduce yourself at a networking event? There is no right or wrong time, only the present. Make the introduction.

In a professional conference/networking/social setting, people expect to mix and mingle. This setting is one where people also expect to meet new contacts, find points of commonality and leave with either a reason to follow up or a friendly face to talk with again at a future time.

Your goal in the first introduction is to meet, make a brief, bright impression and be gone. Don't overstay your welcome and don't approach the conversation to close a deal in that first encounter. Use the analogy that you would not meet someone and propose marriage in the first 10 minutes. Approach networking for the benefit of the relationship, not for "closing" on a meeting, a sale or a bit of advice during the first brief interaction. A "closing" approach is a turn-off to the person you are meeting and it does not create an environment where you are building relationships for future interaction. Remember to be relational and not transactional.

Ryan's Missed Opportunity

The Men's Event is an annual networking and philanthropic gathering that occurs in cities across the country. Hundreds of men gather for dinner and the proceeds benefit prostate cancer research. The following is an example a true story from the 2010 Men's Event.

At the event, a young man named Ryan saw Paul across the room, talking with two friends, the chairman of Ryan's international business and a partner for a leading national firm. Ryan worked for the same company Paul's friend, the chairman, founded and led. However, they had not yet met. Ryan and Paul made eye contact, but his lack of awareness or confidence kept him far enough out of our "circle" that Paul couldn't quietly or easily pull him in. He stood by himself a few feet away from a good conversation. After a few minutes, Paul interrupted his friends and introduced Ryan into the circle. Having had the introduction made, it would have been easy for Ryan to interact with the chairman of his business. However, he froze and had nothing to say. The chairman made a few comments, but Ryan didn't take the bait. The list of attendees was emailed a few days before the event so Ryan could have easily prepared for meeting the chairman of his company. He just stood there and let the opportunity slip away....

Maybe you have found yourself in a similar situation or you see how you could find yourself in a similar situation. If so, it is important to remember that you need to do something to stand out.

The best way to do that is to stand up straight and enter the conversation prepared with a couple of staple comments or questions.

We would advise Ryan to review the attendee list before arriving to see who will be at the event, so he can plan ahead for whom he wants to meet. He could also plan for conversations with those he already knows and will want to talk with.

Once he finds himself in the situation where he sees someone he knows and is standing in sight with the obvious signal that he would like to join the conversation, he should step in and approach the circle. Without being loud or interrupting conversation, he could present himself and trust that Paul will introduce him. If, by chance, the introduction doesn't naturally take place, Ryan would be ready to pardon the interruption and introduce himself. However, in most instances, others are welcoming and will ask questions or allow newcomers into the circle while conversation continues.

Use simple questions to begin conversations with others in a networking setting. For instance, *"I'm a college student and I'm interested in business development within healthcare. Tell me about your healthcare business. What issues are you currently facing? What segments of healthcare do see as having the most growth?"*

You don't want to appear to be interviewing others or rapidly questioning those in the circle, but stating that you are a college student is a terrific entry and lead-in for conversation. As a college student, your willingness to be in the room speaks highly of you.

Once you ask a question, you'll find whether an individual engages with you or does not. If so, let the conversation take its natural course for a few minutes. You can close the conversation by saying, "I am interested in meeting others in the room this evening. Who would you recommend I meet, or is there anyone you might be willing to introduce me to?"

What if my desired contact is talking to someone else?

If there is someone you want to meet at a networking session, but that person is talking intently with someone else, do not interrupt. Use your judgment and when in doubt, hold off on the introduction. Stay close and talk with someone else. Don't stalk your contact, of course, but wait until the conversation softens in intensity or he ends the conversation to walk up confidently and introduce yourself with direct eye contact, a smile and a firm handshake. While you need to communicate well and have a purpose for the introduction, don't feel like you need to control the conversation or provide your life story in the first few moments of the introduction. Sometimes less is more.

The body language you send with a smile, eye contact and a firm handshake can make a profound impression, often much greater than anything you can say. Don't underestimate the power of a first impression.

Once you do make the introduction, be succinct and be gone. If the person you are meeting is alone, he may be able to be more engaged with you if there are not others there he is trying to meet. If you find him asking questions, enjoy the conversation. If you sense that he is also trying to network, you can ask a couple of questions and then end the conversation with, "It is a pleasure to meet you and I appreciate your time. I have a few other thoughts/questions and wonder if I can follow up with you by phone?" If the person is satisfied with this initial conversation ending and having a follow-up conversation, he should provide a confirmation statement and contact information, probably an email address or an assistant's contact information. This is gold. However, if you do receive contact information with permission to follow up, don't be too quick in your follow-up. For instance, if you meet someone on a Thursday night, we suggest you phone or email the following week, maybe the following Monday so you can give it a couple of days. However, you're recent enough that they will remember you and recognize your timely follow up. You can call to say that you enjoyed the meeting and you look forward to a few brief minutes in follow-up.

If you have time flexibility, you can ask if he prefers to talk by phone or in person. If by phone, set the time and do not be late in calling at the confirmed time. Nothing will hurt your credibility more than missing a scheduled call. The phone call allows you to have a prepared list of three to five questions. If the person engages and continues the conversation, that's terrific. If not, it's a good time to wrap up and end the call.

You may be asking, "When can I talk about my career search?" During this phone call or an in-person meeting is a fine time. Know that the person you're talking with is interested in you by the fact that he is willing to spend a few minutes with you. As a result, he is thinking whether he can help you in your search.

Most professionals understand why a job seeker is pursuing a conversation. However, asking a direct question regarding employment is fine. By this phone call or in-person meeting, you have probably talked briefly about your education, your interests and your career pursuits. Therefore, it is reasonable to ask, "I have enjoyed our conversation and appreciate your time. I am looking to (*insert here*) and I would like to ask you for the names of one or two people I should connect with either to either network or to pursue opportunities specific to my interest?"

Avoid asking questions that can be answered with a simple "no" answer. For instance, if you ask if they are hiring, they can say "no." If you ask if there are others they would suggest you talk with, again, they can say "no." Instead, ask open-ended questions. This allows the person to think about his own business, as well as the business professionals he knows, which takes the onus off him to let you down gently because he is still able to help your progress.

By this point in your timeline, you should have researched this person's company and you may know competitors, suppliers and vendors. You may also have a list of specific companies or geographies you are pursuing. If this person has a role for you, explore that first and with focus. If he indicates a willingness to help you network, provide two or three companies you are targeting. This focuses your contact and gets his mental wheels moving as to whom he knows and how they can assist you in networking. Remember that the person you are meeting with has also been where you are, so be prepared, have a few guiding ideas and thank him for any contacts provided.

Practice prepares you for success. Steps you can take include the following:

1. **Practice leaving voice messages to yourself.** Analyze your messages for "ums" and "uhs" and anything that you think detracts from the impact of the message or detracts from you.

2. **Practice in low-stakes environments.** The best way to learn to play golf is to swing the club. Practice introducing yourself to people you don't know in order to become more comfortable and confident. Practice your timing and poise. Practice your entrance, your message, your exchange and your exit. Be engaged, be memorable and be gone. When you're working on networking, you just need to get out there and talk with people. Talk casually with the people next to you in line. Talk to people at the gym. Learn what works for you and what doesn't, what leads to smooth exits and what bungles attempted entrances.

3. **Talk with colleagues, classmates and business professionals.** What has worked for them? What have they seen succeed or fail? Are there nuances or personal or organizational preferences (or even cultural differences) that you can be aware and observant of that will set you apart from the competition?

4. **Create practice scenarios.** What would you do if the CEO of your top target company were standing in front of you at your college or university or was next to you on the driving range? Would you handle those two instances differently? Of course you would, so you can see the importance of scenario work. The entrances are difference, the level of formality might be different and your exit is most certainly different. Being sensitive to these nuances and prepared for their impact is key to your success.

5. **Go where your audience is.** Trade association events, college job fairs, alumni association, non-profit events, chamber of commerce events and industry conferences are generally great places to go to find your audience.

6. **Dress for your audience.** When in doubt, men and women should revert to the standards: men can turn to a suit with a tie or slacks and a jacket with a tie, and women can choose an appropriate-length skirt with a blouse, nice shoes and simple jewelry. Most business events are "business attire" (read: "suit") so plan to

dress the part. In general, the idea is to be "+1" level of formality or polish *above* the environment in which you plan to be.

This "+1" concept ensures that you will be neither over-dressed nor under-dressed. You will stand out, but not stick out. In many settings, men can get away with not wearing a tie; however, there is a high likelihood that you will look like a college student. Since you are striving to be perceived as an up-and-coming business professional, don't risk it by being under-dressed.

It's common for men to interview in a suit and tie. However, many businesses are now "business casual," so men can wear a suit with no tie or slacks and a sport coat and still be "+1." Similarly, women can wear more colorful or artful clothing combinations and still be appropriately dressed with clean shoes and creative jewelry.

Dress is vitally important because it's the first thing your targeted audience will see when they meet you. Also, it's the last thing they will see after talking with you. It carries implications about your respect for an environment, your personal habits, your confidence and even your abilities (as unfair as that may seem). Dress is important and it takes practice, so spend some time getting comfortable in your attire. Spend time observing the people whose career or character you admire. What are they wearing? Remember that your attire sends a message.

7. **Remember that networking is a bit like dating. You wouldn't ask to marry someone during the first date.** You are getting to know one another, getting a sense of possible rapport and making rapid decisions about the other person. Remember, you should be aware of your appearance, tone and style, the questions you ask and the meeting's objective. You need to practice looking the part, sounding the part, filling the part and demonstrating poise in your ability to communicate.

YOUR CHAMPION'S MARGIN TAKEAWAY(S):

_____

_____

_____

_____

_____

_____

_____

CHAPTER 10

Research: Get Smart in 20 Minutes

"The general who wins the battle makes many calculations in his temple before the battle is fought. The general who loses makes but few calculations beforehand."

—SUN TZU

WHETHER YOU ARE trying to learn about an industry (or
industries) as you think about your career interests and pursuits,
or preparing for a company interview, you will have to uncover
and organize meaningful information.

By surveying the industry you will be able to find information and data for one specific company or a range of comparable
companies. We have provided two detailed examples of industry
and company research, which will help you clarify and understand your career interests and company interviews.

Annual Report and Filings: The first stop in researching publicly traded companies is the annual report, a summary of financial
performance, management overview, leadership changes and an
outlook for the next year.

Form 990: The "990" is the non-profit equivalent to an annual
report. It shows the health of the organization through financial
statements, fundraising for the year, capital campaigns, endow-

ment changes, large-scale capital projects and a range of compensation figures.

Trade Associations: These industry-specific groups are a great source for information, conferences, seminars, educational opportunities and collaboration between companies and practitioners. Occasionally they have lobbying agendas that you can research through the public record, but your best asset here is industry information, news and discussions with trade association staff, board of directors and industry members. As a student or young professional, you will have access to the information you need regarding your possible path.

Industry Comparables: You can research and compare degree, experience or skill set requirements for a functional role across multiple industries. You can also learn what a certain job may pay through online job search sites.

Colleagues and Classmates: Find friends, alumni, professional colleagues and acquaintances who can help you get an understanding of the opportunities that exist in your area of interest.

A little bit of focused research can go a long way toward answering questions about whether or not to pursue a particular career path. In fact, that "due diligence" work can often be done in 20 minutes.

Our examples below provide you with real-world how-to pursuits to determine the viability of an opportunity. A thorough approach allows you to investigate a company's performance within an industry and gives you the knowledge and insights to prepare for a mid- to final-round interview in which you will need to ask informed and seasoned questions.

The sidebar features the results of 20 minutes of research in advance of a job interview with Arrington Vineyards, a boutique vineyard in Williamson County, TN. Prior to an interview with this small-production vineyard, you would find limited public information about this vineyard. However, a focused research method can provide you with great baseline industry information and the proper framework to have a meaningful discussion with the interviewer.

While you may not have an interest in working for a small-production vineyard, this example serves as a model of what information you can find on a small niche business in a condensed timeframe. The same method can produce equally valuable information across industry spectrums, so it can be applied to any interview research.

SMART RESEARCH EXAMPLE #1:

Small/Independent Enterprise: Arrington Vineyards (Nashville, TN)

The following information was found in 20 minutes of computer research using a search engine. We didn't talk with anyone in the spirits, wine or beer industry. We didn't talk with anyone employed by or associated with Arrington. You would, of course, find more specific or validating information if you were able to talk with industry people. However, we want to demonstrate the research you can do and the information you can find in a short and focused amount of time.

This information is helpful in your decision process, and we can assure you that starting an interview with the following points will set you apart from the masses of new college graduates interviewing for similar positions.

We've organized the information into bulleted buckets that are meant to offer you a template for your own investigations from this point forward. The information available on the Arrington Vineyards website includes: About Us, Shopping, Calendar of Events and News. As you can see, smaller company's websites tend to have more limited information, hence the challenge. We used an Internet search engine to identify industry issues that would frame up a business discussion with this smaller company.

Industry Overview: What is the 30,000-foot view of this specific market?

- Alcohol, at highest sales levels to date, accounts for over $215B in 2011, up another 10% from 2010's $196.8B.
- The 50 largest companies generate more than 80 percent of revenue.
- Industry has grown by two strategies: Consolidation and restructuring.
- Number of consumers reaching legal drinking age has risen steadily in recent years, based on U.S. Census data.

Conversational Understanding—Questions You May Ask:

- How does a smaller producer like Arrington Vineyards differentiate from the major brands?
- How has this economy impacted customers' purchases of Arrington's wines?
- How much of your wine is being purchased online?

Industry Trends:

- Wine Sales—Positive Outlook:
  - Premium wine will increase sales due to number of consumers over age 55 that consume more wine and prefer premium wine. Three segments:
    - Popular Premium ($6 to $12/bottle retail)
    - Super Premium ($12.01 to $15/bottle)

- Ultra Premium (more than $15)
- Table wine is most popular and fastest-growing type of wine in U.S. Cabernet sauvignon is the most popular variety and white zinfandel is most popular of blush wines.

Understanding Your Interviewers' Top Priorities:

- CEO: Building distributor networks and developing growth strategies.
- COO: Managing winery and vineyard operations and relationships with growers.
- CFO: Negotiating contracts with growers and maintaining liquidity.
- CIO: Automating regulatory monitoring and tracking data.
- HR: Retaining enologists and hiring seasonal labor.
- Sales: Identifying new market segments and advertising to end-users.
  - Brand strength, market position and business mix.

Industry Takeaways:

1. This is a highly consolidated business where large producers control significant portions of the market.

2. People appear to continue to consume alcohol, even in tight economic times. The quality of individual alcohol purchases tends to reflect individual income levels.

Researching an industry of interest or preparing for an interview with a niche private company requires more thoughtful planning when it comes to research, resources and the depth of information available. This creates work in trying to find a healthy amount of industry research and information, as we demonstrated above. Compare this with multinational publicly traded organizations and you will find that you can access tremendous amounts of company and industry information from various resources when the competitive pool gets deeper.

SMART RESEARCH EXAMPLE #2:

Large/Public Enterprise: Target Inc.

It doesn't take long to learn a lot. The issue in researching public companies is that you will need to be focused and clear in navigating through volumes of information to find the information you want and need.

Knowing this, we took a large public company, Target Inc., and spent 20 minutes researching the company's website. Through the Target Investor page, and in just 20 minutes, we found a tremendous amount of information such as Corporate Overview, Stock and Annual Filings, Presentations and News. The following points of information were available about the discount retailer:

Industry Overview: What is the "30,000-foot" view of this specific market?

- Almost $400B annual sales in the industry.
- Wal-Mart and Target are #1 and #2, respectively.
- Due to economic pressure, slowed growth (worth noting).
- Expanded implementation of "Super Stores."

Conversational Understanding—Questions You May Ask:

- "How has this economy impacted customer's purchasing behavior?"
- "How has the sales volume for daily-use items changed over the past year?"
- "How much is online shopping growing?"
- "Can you tell me about the outlook for 2012?"
  - 1,700 entry-level openings in 2012 predicted (major hiring force).
  - Industry-leading leadership development program designed for top talent.
  - 1,750+ retail outlets in the U.S. alone.

Industry Trends:

- "How are private label products growing within Target?"
- "How does Target attract college students?"

Understanding Your Interviewers' Top Priorities:

- CEO: Industry competitiveness, quarterly performance and cost management.
- COO: Logistics, procurement, fulfillment, inventory and systems & process improvement.
- CFO: Contracts with source companies, maintaining liquidity (ensuring enough capital is on-hand for continued investment) and quarterly performance reporting.
- CIO: Managing inventory and limiting "shrink" via RFID or other tech solution.
- HR: Attracting and retaining top talent to a discount-retailing giant.
- Sales: Identifying new market segments and advertising to end-users.

Industry Takeaways:

1. This is a massive industry controlled by a handful of discount retailers.
2. Profitability is based on high-volume, low-margin sales.
3. Price plays a major role in customer loyalty.
4. Rolling out a Target-branded credit card incentive program should appeal to loyalists and attract a number of new patrons.

With your research complete, you have a strong baseline understanding of the industry and company. This knowledge prepares you for an engaging and positive interview experience. You will definitely outshine a majority of the other interviewees.

YOUR CHAMPION'S MARGIN TAKEAWAY(S):

_____

_____

_____

_____

_____

_____

_____

_____

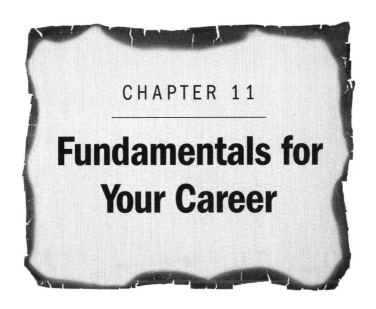

CHAPTER 11

Fundamentals for Your Career

"Success is neither magical nor mysterious. Success is the natural consequence of consistently applying the basic fundamentals."

—JIM ROHN

IT IS IMPORTANT to develop a basic set of fundamental business skills. We believe you should develop these skills in supporting your career decisions. In order to learn how to apply the basics of business, think about the following:

- ❑ What is this company's service or product offering?
- ❑ How does the company generate revenue?
- ❑ What is the financial health of the company?
- ❑ What are the operations that go into delivering the product or service?
- ❑ What key expenses are incurred through delivery? How does the company earn profit?

The six business principles we discuss are: Sales, Accounting and Finance, Marketing, Operations, Communication and Leadership. Follow this outline below to start thinking like a professional.

Accounting and Finance: How does a business track and communicate financial activities? What must the company account for?

- **Revenue – Expenses = Profit**
    - The difference between revenue and profit is important. In its simplest form, revenue is an entity's total inflow of money from operations and profit is the money left over after you pay all expenses.
    - What expenses are incurred in delivering the company's product or service?
    - When does the product or service create company profit? When does the product or service break even and how does profit grow after reaching break-even? For example, a software product has high development costs. However, once break-even is achieved, the profitability per sale is very high.
    - The balance sheet provides you with a snapshot of a company's financial health. The three components of the balance sheet are: assets (what the entity owns), liabilities (what the entity owes) and equity (what the entity is worth). Assets equal liabilities plus equity. Another way to put it is: assets must 'balance' liabilities plus equity.
    - What can your company do to improve company profits? What can you do?
    - Can you look at a competitor's financial statement or

SEC filing and think about where their service may vary, as well as how this impacts pricing strategy and profitability?

Marketing: How are customers identified, targeted and attracted to make a purchase?

- **Size the Market**—What is the market's potential? How many widgets can you sell or how many companies will want to buy your service?
- **Product Definition**—How is the company's product new and/or different from competition? Differentiate relative to the 4 Ps of marketing:
  - *Product*: Consider smart phones and the difference between the 'old' cell phone that simply made a phone call and those that offered texting options. The product evolved. Products also evolved from providing phone, email and text to providing Internet access, video capability, and apps. What's next?
  - *Pricing*: Let's think about your college textbooks. While important, we generally don't view pricing as a long-term differentiator. However, a company must determine a service or product price, which will impact demand and profitability objectives. For example, the same college textbook will cost more, both in production cost and sales cost, in hard-copy

form versus e-book form. Continuing the hard copy versus e-book comparison, the profitability of the e-book is much greater. The e-book achieves break-even more quickly and the subsequent profitability of each additional e-book unit is often greater than the hard copy book. However, the company must determine which version to sell or how many of each version they expect customers to buy.

- *Placement*: Placement is where and how the customer can purchase a desired good or service. Consider Starbucks and Dunkin' Donuts when thinking through the importance of placement. Both companies serve a high-quality product in a clean atmosphere where loyal, regular customers feel a connection to the product, the store and the people who serve them. Customers don't have to look far to get their coffee at either company. Both companies offer retail locations, shops in airports and shopping malls, and their products can be found in grocery stores.

  Consider Southwest Airlines as another example. The Internet put the power of travel in the customer's hands and Southwest Airlines has taken a leadership position in leveraging the Internet to interact with their market. Southwest Airlines provides the ability to engage through a Web browser or smart phone app to book and modify reservations, monitor flight status and check-in. In doing so, many travelers began to see ways to leverage the travel experience with their smart phone. As more and more customers convert to and rely on smart phones, Southwest Airlines and other companies will continue to listen, look ahead and develop new apps to deepen smart phone engagement.

- *Promotion*: The manner by which a customer learns about your product or service is important. Marketers work to build destination websites to link with partners, network through sites aimed at a specific audience or develop search engine optimized (SEO) websites. Referrals and word-of-mouth are the most powerful forms of promotion; however, there are many avenues by which companies share their message. Think about the vast number of sources: friends, family and peers, television, radio and mail, Internet, email and social media, outdoor signage and other public advertising.

- **Market Segmentation**
  - Where are your customers? Market segmentation is about knowing where to find your target customer group. The market for Burn Your Resume is current college students and their parents. College students are motivated and interested in identifying and pursuing interesting career paths, and parents are equally motivated to assist and help students in

finding a job. Therefore, marketing efforts will focus on these two groups.

Sales: How does a business sell a service or product?

- Think from the customer's perspective:
  - Who is the customer?
  - Does the customer need or want this product?
  - Is this a relational or transactional sale?
  - At what prices will the customer buy?
  - What can the salesperson do to drive sales? What can be done to improve the profitability of a sale?

Operations: How does a business operate?

- **Gain understanding of production, distribution and quality**
  - Are operations centralized or decentralized? What is the production schedule? What is the process flow? How do we find and minimize waste in the system?
- **Know the impact of fixed and variable costs**
  - What can be done to reduce variability or improve process controls to improve the profitability margin?
  - Let's look at Arrington Vineyards, which is based in Nashville. Wine often consists of grapes from several vineyards from different regions, such as Washington, Napa Valley, Sonoma and even Middle Tennessee. The first stages of wine production may occur at the vineyard, but the barrels containing the fermenting

wine are often transported to other locations or states for extended periods of fermenting and production. Additionally, the wine may be produced, bottled and prepared in other locations. Staffing, planting, caring for the grapes, harvesting and business operations are central to the vineyard, although the full lifecycle of winemaking may occur across a broader geography. Technology utilization is important to profitability, staffing levels matter greatly and contract negotiating for wine bottling and distribution are very important. The actual growing, production and distribution processes and locations affect operations and profitability.

- Another example is Sweet Cece's, a Nashville-based yogurt franchisor. Paul, a self-professed ice cream and soft-serve yogurt aficionado, is frustrated when ice cream servers skimp on the serving size of his favorite dessert. Dessert volume matters to Paul because he simply loves ice cream. Sweet Cece's resolves Paul's issue by allowing customers to serve themselves the desired volume of yogurt and toppings. There is no volume criterion other than the size of the cup. In this model, the customer pays by weight of serving—and Paul feels satisfied with the experience because he got exactly what he wanted. Although unsubstantiated, we believe this is a highly profitable model. Regarding operations, Sweet Cece's does not produce their own product and their operation includes retail space and a few hourly employees to provide friendly service, maintain a very clean environment, monitor yogurt and topping levels and complete customer purchases. While profitable if done well, this model can be duplicated and therefore the barrier to entry is low. Think about the number of ice cream and frozen yogurt stores in the marketplace and you can see those who know what the customer is actually buying. One of the strengths that Sweet Cici's possesses is system efficiency and consistency, which has resulted in good operations that drive profitability.

Communication—How do you deliver your message?

Another easy way to stand out is something that too many young people overlook: having and using effective communication skills. You need to be able to communicate like an eighth-grader. This means you should be able to demonstrate a strong competency of grammar, spelling and punctuation in your written communications.

Hiring managers and business leaders today complain that their employees cannot write. The concept of effective written communication is changing at different rates in different generations. Many of today's business leaders tend to be of the Baby Boom Generation, who grew up without using email, cell phones or text messaging. Keep other generations in mind when sending emails or making contact through email, and be attentive to spelling, grammar and punctuation because it matters to the people who matter to you.

Whether we like to admit it or not, we judge and are judged by others based on the use of language. Vocabulary, grammar usage and the ability to articulate complex thoughts can make or break communication. The memo is the major leagues of professional communication, offering one page for summarizing information and making recommendations for action.

Start working on your ability to write simple and clear sentences, and "trim the fat" of flowery, loose, verbose or vague language. The ability to boil down a complex issue and make a compelling case on one page is an important skill that should be practiced for maximum impact.

Memo Template:

To:

From:

Date:

Subject:

Summary Paragraph: Explain what you're going to tell them

Body 1: Explain Problem/Issue/Topic

Body 2: Explain Three Possible Solutions

Body 3: Explain Your Recommended or Preferred Course of Action

Conclusion: Summarize what you told them and ask for either approval or their thoughts.

Internships:

Developing knowledge and experience, and speaking the language of business, is important. These business principles are the foundation to your career and we believe you should find as many opportunities as possible to gain practical experience.

Internships are increasingly important for young people who aspire to exceptional careers. Internships expand your knowledge and provide real-world experience to help you develop and determine your career pursuit. An internship allows you to distinguish yourself during college. Internships offer you the opportunity to gain the skills and knowledge that hiring managers understand and require.

Fortunately, internships are widely available across a broad range of industries and job functions. In addition to an internship, you can learn these skills by obtaining a part-time job, starting a small business, serving as a research assistant, leading student government, captaining an athletic team, volunteering for "Alternative Spring Break" or many other opportunities, including mentoring local school children.

Internships also offer the chance to "try before you buy" because you and an employer are given a chance to essentially audition without an extended commitment or real exposure to extensive risk. You and the employer will see how you work, utilize resources, mesh with the team and handle the environment. Carol Bartz, former CEO of Yahoo, highlights another benefit of internships: "[You can] go find out how companies run."

Ways to find great internship opportunities are:

1. Search online
2. Look at *Fortune, INC,* or *Businessweek* magazines for their lists of "Best Places to Launch a Career"
3. Talk with peers, professors, alumni and other university networks
4. Visit your college's career management center

Whether you pursue a paid or unpaid formal internship, a part-time job or a full-time job, real-world work experience will help determine what you're good at and what you enjoy doing. It will also help you develop your skills and meet professionals working full-time in an industry you are considering.

You will set yourself apart with the experience, insights, professional development and relationships you build through an internship.

YOUR CHAMPION'S MARGIN TAKEAWAY(S):

_____

_____

_____

_____

_____

_____

_____

_____

_____

CHAPTER 12

Powerful Interview Preparation

"If I had eight hours to chop down a tree, I'd spend six
sharpening my ax."

—ABRAHAM LINCOLN

B E TRUE TO YOURSELF. It is easy to sit across from an interviewer at a target company and try to craft your answers based on what you think he wants to hear. We have all been there. In retrospect, it is easy to understand why one feels pressure to be the "right candidate" rather than to reverse the equation and search for the right opportunity.

When the employment landscape feels overwhelming or intimidating, it is easy to feel pressure to land a job. That is why we are adamant about helping you align your passions, strengths, interests and values in your job search. We want you to avoid sitting in an interview and trying to present yourself in a way that you think will portray you as an ideal candidate even when you know you aren't a good fit for the organization's culture. In a sense, trying is where we go awry in these situations because it causes us to manufacture an identity.

Be true to yourself in the most professional, polished, prepared and personable way. Putting your best foot forward doesn't mean that you put an inauthentic face on your candidacy. Rather, it just means that you take time to reflect on who you are, what you bring to the table, how you plan to leverage your experience and what you've learned from past mistakes. The key is to be thoughtful and earnest in your preparation so that you can be transparent and authentic in the moment.

A great way to help prepare for an interview is to do your research before you arrive for an interview of any stage, whether that is on the phone, in person or on the final round.

Research: You can learn a lot in 20 minutes

As we demonstrated earlier, you can gain valuable depth and breadth of insight with just a small amount of research ahead of time. The topics are the same and the hot buttons are consistent throughout your search and interview process.

We've provided the following outline for you to follow during your 20-minute research blitz. Find out the answers to these questions so you can prepare yourself for insightful conversation when you have your contact on the phone or during your interview.

This research outline is broken down by theme, with subheadings to help you organize the information in your head:

1. **Industry Overview**
   a) New trends.
   b) Industry sales figures.

    c) External forces.

    d) Identify the top companies.

    e) Common industry growth strategies.

2. **Situational Understanding**

    a) Current state of business?

    b) What does the future look like?

3. **Industry Trends**

    a) What accounts for the top sales sources?

    b) Where is there opportunity to increase market share?

4. **Understanding Your Interviewers' Top Priorities**

    a) **CEO:** Developing growth strategies

        (1) How has the recent economy influenced the way you think about or approach the business practices of the company?

    b) **COO:** Managing business operations and vendor relationships

        (1) Where is the greatest opportunity for operating improvements?

    c) **CFO:** Ensuring accurate financial reporting and managing cash

        (1) How are the variables that impact cash?

        (2) How has the economy impacted your business?

    d) **CIO:** Leveraging technology to drive operations

        (1) What is your stance on social media?

        (2) How do you utilize social media in your operations?

    e) **HR:** Managing human capital

        (1) What is the attrition rate and why do employees leave?

        (2) How do you differentiate your company as an employer of choice?

    f) **Sales:** Segmenting the market and driving revenue

        (1) Do you have an internal sales team or do you leverage partners or distributors?

        (2) How do you analyze new markets?

5. **Industry Takeaways**

    a) What is the current state of the industry?

    b) What are the industry projections?

    c) How is online shopping impacting sales across the industry?

    d) What challenges or advantages exist with regard to government regulations?

In chapter 10, we discussed the interviewers' top priorities for both Arrington Vineyards and Target. That model was meant to give you an advantage when preparing for interviews. We want to help you prepare so you avoid failing to set yourself up to seize the opportunity.

Engaging and meaningful questions can be a major point of differentiation in your interview experience, however formal or informal it may be. A well-timed, well-placed, well-phrased question can identify you as a thoughtful, insightful, curious and engaged candidate.

Practice this with your friends, in front of the mirror, on the phone with your parents, and in the CMC with your career counselor. Unless you practice, it will sound forced. The purpose here is to use questions as a way to build familiarity and rapport with your target interviewer. Then, with that as a foundation, you will begin to position yourself as a winning candidate.

YOUR CHAMPION'S MARGIN TAKEAWAY(S):

_____

_____

_____

_____

_____

_____

_____

_____

CHAPTER 13

Standing Out

"First say to yourself what you would be, then do
what you have to do."

—EPICTETUS

To THIS POINT, you have put time and effort into preparing for interviews. We will now focus on how you should set your mind, communicate, present and separate yourself.

Positive Mental Attitude

Preparation builds confidence and confidence allows you to relax and feel comfortable with the plan you prepare for your interview. A positive attitude is critical. You have real leverage when you believe in yourself and demonstrate outward confidence and a positive approach to the discussion.

Many authors of sales and self-help books encourage readers to practice positive self-affirmations such as, "I am a strong candidate and I will have a good day today by speaking knowledgeably, clearly and with energy." We believe in the power of your mind and have seen it work in our own lives. If perception is reality, it is up to you to create the confidence and self-efficacy necessary to succeed and achieve.

The candidate who repetitively thinks and states positive thoughts prior to an interview is like the boxer who wakes up at 2 a.m. every day to do sets of push-ups and sit-ups. When you ask the boxer why he does this he says, "Because I know my competition is sleeping." When the pugilists meet, the more prepared and affirmed boxer stands a better chance of winning. This applies to interviews and business meetings, too. If you are prepared, and if you have convinced yourself of your plan and what outcome you want from the meeting, you'll be astonished to see that your reality can be what you believed and affirmed for yourself.

Optimism

Believe in good outcomes. This doesn't mean that you'll always have positive outcomes. Actually, we can assure you that you will not have consistently positive outcomes. However, an optimistic person is compelling to others and tends to find opportunities, even when the initial window of opportunity has been closed. The pessimist repels people and the optimist attracts. Be an optimist.

Energy

A car that is not cared for will not last long or perform well. Maintain a regular exercise program to keep your body well tuned. Energy is contagious and people want to work with individuals who have an energetic approach to their work. Layer positive energy on top of your optimistic outlook as you pursue your opportunities.

Body and Facial Language

Even if you don't feel confident, you can appear so by simply doing these three things: stand up straight, smile and get your hair out of your eyes so you can make eye contact. Good posture and attentiveness shift the dynamic of a situation in your favor.

Listening versus Talking

During an interview, strive for a balance of listening versus talking. Usually that will be 50/50, although some interviewers strive to talk more to you, while others ask more questions and expect you to do most of the talking. In those cases, you will either interrupt your interviewer or awkwardly ask your interviewer questions while he is trying to pull information from you.

Don't force the conversation to a 50/50 balance, but be aware. If you find that the culture of the company is consistently one where all the interviewers dominate the conversation—or all interviewers say little and expect you to do all of the talking—put your corporate culture antennae up. Companies that don't allow you to talk may be working hard to sell their company or they may be telling you that they don't value input from new graduates. Employers who don't engage with you or answer your questions may have a defensive culture or one by which individual performance and knowledge is the only benchmark for success. These are not rules or guarantees, but they may help you avoid a poor fit, so be alert.

Talk in Terms of Team

Interviews are interesting in that much of the working world is built around teams accomplishing goals, while your resume and interview focus exclusively on your individual performance. You can practice highlighting the work of your team in completing a task and your personal role among the team.

Clarity of Message

Be clear. Tell the interviewer what you think the role is about and talk with the interviewer about how you can make a difference. With clarity, brevity is important, as is tone and inflection. You may find that your interview requires or allows you to present your ideas or experience to a group. You will do yourself and your audience a favor if you learn the power of clarity and brevity when presenting.

Learn how to communicate your message in five slides at the most. Using slides to show how smart you are, to define a topic everyone else is aware of, or to restate what people already know is not effective. Your goal is to talk with people and engage people in your message and plan. As a target, think about three to five bullet points you want to share in no more than five slides. By all means, don't read what you have on a projector or computer screen. Your audience can read—you should be able to add color to the bullets or use the points as conversation starters.

Dress for the Interview

"Dress for the job you want, not the job you have," goes the adage. Your attire should be clean and provide a crisp look that marks you as a professional and allows the interviewer to focus on your conversation and not the messiness of your dress.

Right or wrong, you will be perceived by how you dress. If you are not sure about how to dress for an interview, we suggest the "+1" approach. Essentially, take the company's dress code and step it up one notch: "+1." We have offered the guidance, below, separated for women, for men and for both when appropriate in order to make it easier to reference.

Women: You should aim for a polished look that shows the interviewer you were thoughtful and respectful in your dress. Style is fine and should be explored, but you should think about presenting an overall well-groomed and professional look. Look professional and let the interview focus on your abilities, knowledge and personality and how well prepared you are for the meeting.

Women no longer need to defer to old-school dress requirements: a suit, including a skirt and jacket, with a blouse, panty hose or stockings and pearls. For too many young professionals, this is a stiff look that creates a rigid appearance inconsistent with their personality.

Women can be fashionable and professional at the same time by keeping the following fashion tips in mind:

1) Be mindful of necklines and hemlines, and select clothes accordingly.

2) Find suits, mix-and-match pieces and staple garments that fit well, finish well and can be maintained.

3) Be aware of how pants fit, buttons on shirts and appropriate accessories.

4) Pantsuits are professional and can be worn instead of dresses and skirts.

5) Skirts with tights and dress boots are appropriate, especially when complemented by scarf and/or jewelry options.

6) Blouses and shirts need to be dry cleaned and buttoned up. The interview is generally not the time to set new fashion trends.

7) Shoes should be clean and polished. The point of shoes should be polished and not overly scuffed.

Men: We strongly encourage men to wear white undershirts underneath dress shirts. You will get nervous in your interview and you do not want to soak your dress shirt. The undershirt will save you some embarrassment that could negatively impact your interview.

Make sure your belt is appropriate for your outfit and that it matches your shoes. Don't wear a brown belt with black dress shoes.

Ties need to be tied where the front point reaches the top of your belt. Don't go much shorter or you will look like an amateur. Leaving your tie too long is also a mistake, especially if you're less than six-feet tall. As for color, you can have some freedom with this, but we suggest you avoid wild or overly colorful patterns. A tie should complement your hair and facial color because it is meant to transition your suit to your face. A loud tie is distracting; when in doubt, default to solid red or blue. You want the interviewer to focus on your message and see you as clean, crisp and professional.

Shine your shoes. Research has shown that people tend to look at shoes to generate opinions. Don't let your shoes distract from who you are and what you can do for an employer. Also, make sure to wear clean hole-free socks that extend above your calf. Whenever possible, avoid the mid-calf sock. If you cross or fold your leg while seated, the skin on your leg should not show.

Gentlemen, if you find yourself in an environment where you can wear slacks and a jacket, keep similar rules. Go with a pressed white or blue dress shirt. Unless you will be golfing during an interview, do not wear a golf shirt. Select a confident, well-presented tie. Slacks can be grey or khaki with a blue blazer. Avoid pairing black slacks with a blue jacket. If you wear solid black slacks, purchase a jacket that is not solid black or solid blue. There are several patterns that look nice. However, avoid this level of style unless you have financial resources to pay for a credible tailor to help outfit you. Through all of this maintain the same rules regarding your shoes, socks, belt, undershirt and tie. Look sharp and keep people focused on the meeting and not your clothes.

Men and Women: Spending money on nice-looking business casual and business dress attire is a good investment. In fact, spending money on a good suit is a differentiator for corporate roles. With regard to suits, stick with the colors that have survived the test of time: grey, blue, black, or a pinstripe in one of the three previously mentioned colors. We advise wearing a blue or white pressed dress shirt in order to avoid distraction. However, you will find different suggestions and trends based on industry.

Make sure your suit and shirt are pressed, preferably by a local dry cleaner. A crisp look flows nicely; a botched, self-ironed shirt screams out that you are not aware of how to present yourself. Also, many dress shirts require collar stays—don't forget these plastic gems. If you do, your collar will curl up before the day is over, and it's hard to hide the curling collar when everyone looks right at your neck and face.

As for piercings, many employee handbooks rule out nose and mouth piercings. Ladies should remove any piercings other than traditional earrings in the ear lobe. Gentlemen, we recommend removing earrings and piercings. Earrings have become quite popular, but remember your audience and respond accordingly. If you have tattoos on your neck or arms, we suggest you cover them up as much as possible. Use your best judgment.

Let us say again: Whether we like it or not, we are judged by our appearance. This includes the suits we wear, slacks we choose and how they fit, sport coats and whether they're tailored properly, shirts and their collar and cuff combination (spread collar and French Cuffs for a more formal look, tab collars and barrel cuffs for a more traditional business to business-casual look), shoes (thinner soles tend to be more formal, natural materials tend to be more refined) and even socks (no athletic socks!). Keep the following two rules in mind at all times:

RULE #1: **Remember your audience.** Be sure to be sensitive to their priorities.

RULE #2: '+1'. Know the expectations and exceed them by one step.

Industry Attire Guidelines & Suggestions

When in doubt, suit up. Professional business attire is still the best default outfit for a first interview. Subsequent interviews may allow you the opportunity to dress down, but you should dress like a true professional for your first interview. Of course, this rule depends a bit on the industry and the company.

If you are interviewing with a non-profit organization, you

will send the wrong message if you dress in a high-end business suit. The interviewer will read you as being in "interview mode" and therefore not acting as yourself. Additionally, it shows that you have not researched the industry or the business.

Similarly, a woman wearing a skirt suit without pantyhose for a January interview in Chicago or a man wearing a three-piece tweed suit with a bowtie to an August interview in Miami will probably cause the interviewer to question that person's awareness and sensitivity to details. Be aware of your environment and dress appropriately.

The following list provides a general overview of dress codes for various industries:

Finance: Suit up. Go big if you're looking for an opportunity at a top investment bank. Suit, tie, spread collar shirt with French cuffs and polished shoes for men. Suit, pressed shirt, heels, neat hair, makeup and tasteful jewelry for women.

Consulting: Suit up. Though the rule here is generally the same for women in finance, consulting is a possible step down from finance. This means no need to wear French cuffs with your suit. Consulting firms are more open to bold colors or interesting patterns on shirts, depending on the focus. When in doubt, for either gender, go with a crisp white shirt, charcoal or black suit, a splash of color with a tie or accent piece and minimal jewelry (watch, ring). From there, it's up to your best sense.

Operations: If this is a factory position, khakis and a button down shirt may do. However, this is a good opportunity for slacks and a sport coat. Again, your goal is to communicate respect for the interviewer, his or her company, the role and yourself. Be sure to carry yourself with that professional shine.

Marketing and Advertising: Compared to finance and consulting dress requirements, this industry offers more opportunities to dress boldly. However, check out the company's website to understand where their aesthetic boundaries lie. Be true to yourself, but feel free to express yourself, too. This could mean a patterned shirt or a suit with a bold pattern or pinstripe through it. Splashes of color are welcome and, perhaps, expected. Be smart about the patterns and colors you put together. Make sure you possess the flare for style and appropriateness. Incorrectly matching patterns will do more harm than good. If you have the resources and the capacity, dress with creativity.

Non-profit Organizations: Be aware of the type of work a non-profit conducts while considering what to wear to an interview. Be crisp, professional and pulled-together to communicate your interest in the work while also displaying your awareness of the environment.

These examples should equip you to plan for and execute attire decisions that will set you apart from the competition in positive and sustainable ways.

YOUR CHAMPION'S MARGIN TAKEAWAY(S):

_____

_____

_____

_____

_____

_____

_____

_____

CHAPTER 14

Your
Backstage Pass

"Spectacular achievement is always preceded by spectacular preparation."

—ROBERT H. SCHULLER

PREPARING FOR THE COMPANY INTERVIEW

THIS PORTION OF THE BOOK will lay out a series of common interview questions that we have compiled over our years of experience. The following questions are organized and structured as follows: FIRST, what interviewers are sure to ask; SECOND, what the questions mean; and THIRD, what information the interviewers are actually looking for.

This section should help you efficiently and effectively prepare for interviews. You will begin to see patterns and, by the time you're sitting across from your interviewer, you will be able to speak clearly, concisely and directly to their actual interests.

Questions you should expect are in bold with their translated purposes listed below.

1. **Walk me through your resume.**

   a. Show me that your path to this point makes sense. Tell me your coherent and purposeful story.

    b. Do you have an idea, or range of ideas, for what you want to do and what you are capable of doing?

2. **Tell me about a time you had to convince a group about an unpopular plan or idea.**

    a. How do you communicate unpopular, negative or bad news?

    b. Tell me how you handle adversity. Can you rally others?

3. **Tell me about a project you completed as the member of a team. How did you do it? (Use the STAR [Situation, Task, Action, Result] or SAO [Situation, Action, Outcome] method.)**

    a. I want to know if you can play a variety of roles in a collaborative setting and that you are responsible.

    b. Can you clearly articulate your experiences and draw similarities to the interviewer's business, industry or the role you're applying for?

4. **What is the most difficult situation you have been in and how did you respond?**

    a. Prove that you are reflective and self-aware, confident but humble, and that you have standards to measure yourself and your performance.

    b. Convince me that you know how to answer criticism productively and can bounce back from a personal hit.

5. **Have you ever had your personal integrity questioned? How did you respond? What was the outcome?**

   a. Tell me how you've demonstrated character and integrity.

   b. Can I trust you? Show me how you deal with a difficult or uncomfortable question and show me you have reasonable expectations.

6. **Tell me about a time you overcame an obstacle or a setback to achieve something you cared about.**

   a. Prove to me that you have determination and grit. I want someone who knows the value of hard work.

   b. I want to know if you can learn from mistakes and how you respond to regrets or missteps.

7. **If you could redo a day, what day would you choose and how would you change it?**

   a. Demonstrate that you have a clear understanding of how your passions and strengths mesh with daily reality.

   b. Can you reflect on past performance and prior experience to help influence the way you behave, react, engage and address problems, people and tasks?

8. **What do you not want to be? What do you not want to do in a job?**

   a. How interesting is the role and the company you're

interviewing with? Is this something you really want to do and how committed are you?

b. How does the role I'm trying to fill align with your interests and career pursuits?

9. **What would you say is a perfect job for you?**

a. Demonstrate that you have direction.

b. Do you demonstrate a willingness to engage challenging topics?

10. **Where do you see yourself five years from now?**

a. Are you a person who aspires to be more?

b. Are you the kind of person I want on my team?

11. **How much do you expect to be paid for this role?**

a. Do you have a fair sense of your own value to a group?

b. Have you researched market and competitive compensation?

12. **How much do you believe a company should pay for someone like you to accept this role?**

a. Have you demonstrated the ability to successfully deliver results in the past?

b. Do you know your expenses and whether you can "afford" this job?

13. Role Simulation

One example is the classic case study. Until recently, consulting firms primarily used case studies in their interviews. Many of these firms (McKinsey, Boston Consulting Group, Bain & Co. and Deloitte) have case preparation resources on their websites. Books such as *Cracking the Case* can also help you prepare for such an interview.

a. Can you break down problems and make a reasonable suggestion for solving them?

b. Are you a clear and effective communicator?

Be sure to spend a fair amount of time researching your target company's preferred approach to this portion of the interview. The point is to approach business problems from a logical and consistent manner that is recognized and valued by your potential employer.

There are several quantitative, analytical, technical, scenario and simulation assessments that employers use to pre-screen applicants and during the interview process. You should be aware of the company's interview process. You can find this information online, through your CMC, alumni networks, college peers and professors.

YOUR CHAMPION'S MARGIN TAKEAWAY(S):

_____

_____

_____

_____

_____

_____

_____

_____

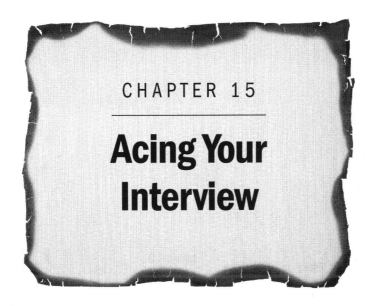

CHAPTER 15

Acing Your Interview

"The people who get on in this world are the people who get up and look for the circumstances they want, and, if they can't find them, make them."

—GEORGE BERNARD SHAW

YOU'VE GOT THE BASICS. Beyond that, when you ask for guidance the most common advice you receive will probably sound something like, "Be yourself." But what does that really mean? Look back a few pages to see what we suggest about being true to yourself, or spend some time thinking about what you're really aiming to achieve on a longer-term scale.

We urge you to be aware of how easy it is to get seduced by the possibility of the short-term opportunity. This is the point we made when we discussed staying true to yourself during interviews. We can be firm in our values, our vision of the future and our passions, yet we can easily find ourselves giving answers we think will impress or satisfy interviewers.

Please know that "Being You" or "Acing the Interview" doesn't always translate to "Getting Hired." The point is this: Be Prepared to Present Yourself Well. You may be wondering, "What does it mean to present well in each interview setting?" Whether you are participating in a phone interview, in-person interview, group interview or even a case interview, we have compiled and distilled some helpful hints for each interview setting.

First, you must turn off your cell phone during an interview. Don't have it on vibrate, don't have it on silent—turn it off. Your top priority throughout an interview should be the interview. You won't answer a phone call, text or email during the interview, so why have it on? If you're interviewing, be focused and interview well. You can email, text and talk on the phone when the interview is over. Remember that you are trying to differentiate yourself from the droves of people around you. Small touches can make a big difference.

FOUR INTERVIEW ROADMAPS

Phone Interviews:

Interviewers may know who you are, but appreciate a refresher at the start of a phone interview. Cover this gap by simply reminding the person who you are, how you learned about the opportunity, what excites you about it and what your goals might be.

Here are some other tips for phone interviews:

1. **Control your Environment.** After you have introduced yourself and essentially framed your candidacy, make sure you continue to speak clearly and with crisp enunciation. There is no bigger frustration on the phone than not being able to hear the interviewee. Don't take your interview call outside on a quiet corner of the main quad. There might be some unexpected traffic and background noise in that area. If this happens, the interview will be awkward, loud and distracting—strikes one, two and three.

2. **Be Clear.** Remember that a major value of the phone interview is efficiency. To that end, you will make yourself memorable if you are efficient in your communication. Offer tight and coherent responses to questions that demonstrate your ability to distill and communicate information.

3. **Be Brief.** Balance talking with listening. However, a 50/50 balance is not always realistic. Some interviewers ask more questions than they expect you to ask or they will spend more time telling you about their business and the role you're interviewing for. Make sure you are being clear and balancing your talking with your questions as much as possible. Remember that you are working to establish a dialogue, not a monologue. To build rapport and be remembered, you have to make sure to ask questions and manage the flow of conversation

as best you can. This will humanize you and help the interviewer imagine you as a colleague.

4. **Know the Process.** Be sure to ask the interviewer about the next steps in the process. Asking communicates that you understand the hiring process. You can tell the interviewer that you would like to continue in the process.

5. **Schedule a Follow-up Conversation.** The sign of a good conversation or meeting is the commitment and scheduling of a follow-up conversation or meeting. While it is not always possible to schedule a firm next step, you want to ask for it because it allows you to understand the timing and the process. It also provides insight into whether you are being considered as a viable candidate.

In-Person Interviews and Group Interviews:

Face-to-face exchanges are a benefit to almost everyone, because human communication is made up mostly of body language, visual cueing and inference. Group interviews and one-on-one interviews are very similar—both require that you separate yourself from the pack. For that reason, it is important that you follow these tips for in-person and group interviews:

1. **Stand Tall.** Posture can make or break you. Standing tall communicates confidence, competence and health. Even if these are subconscious cues, they will impact

other people's sense of you as a candidate and potential
coworker. Look at yourself in the mirror as you slouch,
then stand up straight as if a string is pulling from the top
of your head through the ceiling. Take note of how your
character changes with your silhouette.

2. **Smile and Make Eye Contact.** This communicates
that you are confident, engaging and pleasant. We
connect with people who look us in the eye. Practice
with friends, family, teachers and the people behind the
counter wherever you go until it becomes natural and
comfortable. You will notice the positive impact it has on
your ability to connect with people.

3. **Offer a Firm Handshake.** A handshake tells people a lot
about who you are. Confidence comes through a handshake.
Practice with people you know, people you love, people you
meet and even people who come to install the cable system.
Whatever you do, don't offer the "dead fish" handshake.
Seat the base of your thumb and forefinger firmly in theirs,
flex your hand and squeeze with solid strength similar to
the amount required to pour a two-liter bottle of soda into
a glass. While you're shaking hands, smile and make eye
contact while holding a tall posture.

4. **Passion, Enthusiasm and Engagement.** Bring this
everywhere you go. Project yourself as an optimistic team
player who will bring energy, innovation and passion to
the job. Passion and enthusiasm do not mean you have to

bounce off of the walls or show false outward excitement. It does mean that your words, your actions in preparation and your inner drive to pursue your chosen career are obvious to others.

5. **Always Have Questions.** When an interviewer asks, "Do you have any questions for me?" The answer should always be yes! The following questions communicate your interest in the role and will yield important information. Reference these questions to create a list of your own.

Here is a list of 10 questions you could ask during an interview:

❏ What do you enjoy most about working for (company name)?

❏ Why did you first choose to come to (company name) and what keeps you motivated to stay?

❏ What have some of the most successful people in this type of role done to make a positive impact?

❏ What does a typical day look like for someone in this role?

❏ What does success look like in this role and what are your desired outcomes?

❏ Who are the top three customers in this role, both internally and externally?

❏ What characteristics are you looking for in your top candidates?

❑ What are some of the common challenges in this role?

❑ What is some advice you wish you'd been given at the beginning of your time here? What would have made a difference for you?

❑ Are there any questions I didn't fully answer for you? Is there something we should revisit before we finish?

These questions imply your interest in the opportunity and your interest in adding value immediately to the organization.

6. **For group interviews, talk to all of the interviewees.**
Don't just talk to the interviewer. Part of the reason behind a group interview is to help gauge your ability to work with people you don't know. Always look at the individual who asked the question in the eye. However, include others in the discussion by also looking at them during your responses. You don't have to cover the entire group for each question. Basically, avoid talking only to the person who asks the question. You can engage the group by looking at others as you respond.

This is a great forum for showing your same poise, confidence, optimism, energy and distinction. Don't be pushy, don't be petty, just be yourself and engage the people around you with authenticity. You will need to be able to engage people on a peer-to-peer basis as well as managing a multi-party dialogue about what are sure to be interesting topics.

Trade Show or Career Fair Interview:

Your adrenaline will be charging and your palms will probably be sweaty. You'll be in a sea of people, all similarly qualified and all with similar goals. It is more important than ever to lend yourself context, to offer your points quickly and efficiently, to find a time for your next contact and move on.

Here is the progression:

1. **Introduce Yourself:** Just as with the phone interview, give your interviewer a way to differentiate you from the competition. You want the interviewer to be able to mentally file you as a top candidate.

2. **Eye Contact, Good Posture, Firm Handshake:** As with any in-person exchange, you need to humanize yourself, offer a way for the interviewer to connect with you and give the interviewer a sense of who you are, how you are and what kind of person you might be. Your eye contact, posture and handshake will help you stand out. If you are consistent with your crisp and clear context, your verbalization of wanting to respect their time, and the message you leave, you will be a memorable candidate, regardless of the brevity of your exchange.

3. **Schedule a Follow-Up:** After delivering a message of who you are, what your goals are and why you're excited to be talking to them about an opportunity, you will have a few moments for back-and-forth conversation. Before leaving, make sure to schedule a follow-up meeting or appointment by saying, "I know there are several other people interested in shaking your hand and talking briefly. Thank you for your time. May I please set up another chance to sit down with you or a colleague to discuss this opportunity in greater detail? I like what I've heard and want to do what I can to pursue this position." You have distinguished yourself.

4. **Be Bright, Be Brief and Be Gone:** Your interviewer has scores of people vying for his or her time. Demonstrate your awareness of this by saying something like, "I know your time is valuable, so I'll be as brief as possible." Be bright, be brief and be gone. Your immediate actions— such as a handwritten follow-up note—will build upon a strong start and theme.

Dinner Meetings and Interviews

There are three things to remember when you sit down for a meal with an interviewer: you are there to learn, to share and to make an impression.

Keep the following tips in mind:

1. **You're Not There for the Food.** Don't be indecisive with the menu and don't eat your dinner like you're in an eating contest. Focus on the conversation, on the person across from you and on learning and exchanging information. You should be less inclined to focus on food and more inclined to focus on the discussion.

2. **Focus on the Conversation.** Don't order something that is messy to eat or that will take your attention off the dialogue, such as spaghetti or ribs.

3. **Mind your Manners.** If you have not learned how to eat like a civilized person, it's time to learn. There are hundreds of books written about table manners—it is worthwhile to invest in one. Here are some of the most important practices to keep in mind: how you hold your silverware while keeping your elbows relaxed at your sides; the pace with which you eat; the posture you use during the meal; and the practice of not talking with food in your mouth. Most importantly, remember to maintain comfortable and attentive eye contact with your dinner partner(s).

GENERAL GUIDELINES THAT YOU MUST NOT FORGET:

Never Overlook a Company's Receptionist or Assistant

Don't underestimate or ignore the power of a receptionist or assistant. The person you are interviewing may rely on this individual. This person maintains a calendar, sets privacy levels and boundaries by which people can gain access and filters a tremendous amount of information. Be pleasant, courteous, polite and friendly to receptionists and assistants. Look them in the eye when you talk to them. You will find that some are more engaging than others. If they are engaging, take the cue and engage. It's easy to ask them about the company, how long they have been there, why they like it and the culture of the company and the office. If you are rude to this person or if you discount their ability or influence, you will be badly mistaken and will have made a poor choice. Many hiring managers solicit input from receptionists to help them decide whom to hire based on how candidates engage with people they don't think are "important." Treat everyone with whom you come into contact with genuine and sincere professionalism respect.

Alcohol: Just Say No

Regardless of your age, avoid alcohol during any interview, whether it's at an office, over a meal, at a sporting event or at the local diner. Others may choose to drink, but we suggest you avoid alcohol in these settings and environments. There is nothing wrong with saying no to ordering a beer, glass of wine or a drink.

Once you are hired and brought into social settings, alcohol may be available. In social environments, it may feel like you should join in the drinking. However, if you are hesitant or don't want to drink, be confident enough to stand firm and say, "No, thank you." Ask for bottled water, a soft drink, club soda or iced tea instead. You may believe that you can be cautious and still enjoy a beer or drink, but we advise that you avoid this. As a new employee, people are forming opinions about you based on your interaction, ability, performance and social skills.

You want to demonstrate your restraint and maturity, and passing on having a beer does not put you in a bad light. Everything you do sends a message about who you are as a potential colleague and company representative. Make sure you stay on top of that message.

POST-INTERVIEW, FOLLOW-UP AND FOLLOW THROUGH:

1. The Art of the Thank You Note

You are finished with your interview and now you want to follow up in a meaningful and differentiating manner. Now is the time to ice the deal with a succinct and sincere thank you note. The purpose is to provide another way to stand out in the minds of your interviewers. Your note can be as simple as:

"Dear (*insert here*),

Thank you for taking the time to speak with me on Tuesday. I enjoyed meeting you and the team. (*Pull out one or two points from your discussion that you can comment on directly, such as:)* Arrington Vineyard's decision to expand the distributor base is exciting and I would enjoy helping you to identify, contact and pursue those relationships. I look forward to hearing from you.

Thank you,

Signature"

This is short, direct and sincere. Add your own flavor to your note, but the point is to communicate your gratitude and be sure the people responsible for your interview are reminded of your enthusiasm and consideration.

The thank you note is a subtle touch that receives significant recognition—even in the 21st century. The thank you note is a great way to stand out. Take five minutes to hand-write a note to someone, whether that person served to put you in touch with a potential employer, took a few hours out of their day to offer advice or a sympathetic ear, or sent a gift to welcome you to the area. The handwritten note has no substitute when it comes to being noticed. We encourage you to use professional stationery or notecards for these instances. Thank-you notes don't have to be long or overly involved, but should be sincere, concise and relevant.

2. Focused Follow-up and Thorough Follow-through

If you find yourself in the position of not hearing anything for an extended period—more than two weeks following your interview or whatever amount of time your interviewer set—feel free to follow up with a professional email or voicemail message. Use the opportunity to reiterate your interest, tell what you gained from your interview experience and express your desire to help advance the process however you can. This is you trying to be helpful, not you being pushy. Be professional, succinct and pleasant. Practice this to be certain.

Make no more than three attempts to reconnect with a company. After the second attempt, make a third and final attempt to connect. We suggest you do this by phone and leave a brief, pleasant message explaining yourself and thanking them for their time. The interviewer may reach back out to you at a point in time, but you do not want to become a nuisance.

Bottom Line

This advice is the distillation of years of experience, scores of mistakes and a litany of lessons learned. We urge you to practice your craft until you find the mix that works for you. You will find a pattern and style that works. Know that you are not doing this to perfect your craft, but instead to use action and repetition to develop and refine your career pursuit. We want to provide the outline for your pursuits, but we want you to personalize your approach so that you show your true self.

YOUR CHAMPION'S MARGIN TAKEAWAY(S):

CHAPTER 16

Finding Your Fit

"You will find men who want to be carried on the
shoulders of others, who think that the world owes them
a living. They don't seem to see that we must all lift
together and pull together."

—HENRY FORD

CORPORATE CULTURE is the "feel" of a business or organization. It is made up of the group's dominant personalities, their shared value system, the most highly-prized talents and contributions, the unwritten rules by which the group works and interacts and the general climate within which all of the action (interpersonal and professional) happens.

Corporate culture is a concept that is getting more attention these days. Corporate culture entered the national spotlight during the "dot-com boom" of the late 1990s when Silicon Valley developed and invested in droves of start-up companies whose business models depended more upon technology and remote access than on brick-and-mortar, face-to-face exchanges.

Business dealings during that period shifted from physical to virtual; therefore, dress code became a non-issue and creativity a top priority. This shift appealed to the West Coast culture, as well as to younger people in the work force. It ultimately led to the development of the "converted-warehouse-with-a-ping-pong-table-and-a-video-game-console" company that is synonymous with the dot-com era. This confirmed that the "suit-and-tie" wasn't the only way to do business, and with the clear shift to the power of the Internet, suddenly there was diversity of options for work environments to an unprecedented extent.

Clues to Watch For

During the late 1990s, many companies began to embrace the "business casual" aesthetic as a gesture to workers whom they knew had new options that appealed to their humanity and individuality. Today, companies like Facebook and Zappos are not uncommon in their emphasis on personal fulfillment and comfort at work.

Recent trends indicate that employees of the late Generation Y and early Millennial Generation expect their personal and professional worlds to merge. This does not mean, however, that employers will or should be expected to allow sneakers to work. We are referring to the personality, responsibility and values of an organization.

Attire and dress codes are not the only indicators of corporate culture. Rather, they are helpful tools in deciding what type of place you're dealing with if you have no other information.

Another clue to corporate culture is whether executives are called by their first names or more formal titles. A general guideline is that if your executive team expects to be called "Ms. This" or "Dr. That," you are probably dealing with a structured, formal and competitive culture. The companies that encourage first-name-basis interaction tend to be more egalitarian, more collaborative and less dependent upon hierarchy.

Yet another corporate culture clue is the building design itself. Many cutting-edge, progressive, creative and collaborative organizations rely on open floor plans that encourage communication and a free flow of ideas by their very design. Does the office have a lot of windows or is it a cube farm? Is there art on the walls or is it a blank slate? Is there space to commune and relax during breaks? What food options exist in the space? Do employees work from home or have that option? Do they offer flex hours to attract bright and capable part-time staff? Are there consultants throughout the company or is everyone an employee? What are the meeting spaces like? Pay attention to these details while touring a building to determine if a company offers the type of corporate culture in which you will flourish.

Determining Fit

There are many personality assessments available today to help identify your best corporate fit, from personality tests and color-coded summaries to left-brain/right-brain assertions. However, it comes down to finding the right balance of comfort and challenge for you. Ask yourself the following questions:

- How do current employees talk about the company?
- Do you prefer a formal or informal work environment?

- Would you rather compete or collaborate for success?
- What skills do you think a company should value in its associates?
- Are you interested in developing a creative or analytical skill set?
- How highly does the company you're targeting value your intended role?
- At first blush, does this feel like a company you would enjoy working for?
- To what extent do you see yourself enjoying being around your potential colleagues?

Your answers to these questions will clarify whether you are entering a "shark-tank" or a culture at the other end of the spectrum, where personalities and likeability drive the culture. It's up to you to decide where on the continuum you wish to invest your time and your energy.

The Good and the Bad: Warning Signs

If you feel tense (more than just nervous energy associated with your interview) when you walk through the door, when you meet your potential colleagues, or when you think about joining the group, you might want to reconsider your pursuit and continue your search.

If you get an uncomfortable "gut feeling" from the leaders in your potential company, that could indicate a potentially poor fit because organizations tend to take on the personality of their leadership.

Other signs to watch out for include whether or not the people on your potential team share your sense of humor, whether or not you feel a connection with your potential manager, and whether or not you believe in or are passionate about the mission of the company. If these outcomes are misaligned with your style, you should continue your search.

As long as the good outweigh the bad, and as long as your key priorities aren't violated or compromised, you stand a chance of enjoying and succeeding at your job. A good way to determine your stance is to create a "pros and cons" list on a blank sheet of paper with a line down the middle. If there are more "pros" than "cons," it is probable that you will be in an environment that is a positive match for you.

The opposite is also true about "cons." Be sure to account for the relative weight of each item you write down, however, because there could be certain "non-negotiable" things that would disproportionately tip the scale and clarify your decision.

YOUR CHAMPION'S MARGIN TAKEAWAY(S):

_____

_____

_____

_____

CHAPTER 17

Fielding Your Offer

"Destiny is not a matter of chance; it is a matter of choice. It is not a thing to be waited for; it is a thing to be achieved."

—WILLIAM JENNINGS BRYAN

Compensation

How do you respond when asked about expected or current compensation? If you are approaching graduation, many of your peers will rely on what their career management center tells them is the expected compensation. Unfortunately, many people listen to their friends for information about expected compensation. The worst-case scenario is the individual who relies on information from a friend who was just offered the same job. Following this path for a compensation conversation will lead to a frustrating result because your information is not grounded in objective reality. You need to be proactive in finding accurate information from trusted sources.

How should you talk with an employer about compensation? Remember the adage, "It's often not what you say, but how you say it." Be confident, balance your emotions and approach the conversation with the idea that you will probably work with and know the other person for several years to come. Asking for a specific salary or compensation range is common in the business world. It is not a guaranteed path to receiving what you ask for, but it frames your expectations.

Receiving an Offer

For a new college graduate, receiving an employment offer is an exciting time. However, negotiating the job offer can also be stressful. Are you expected to know what you should be paid? Are you expected to negotiate and ask for a certain salary? If you are provided an offer, is it acceptable to negotiate? Is it expected? The bottom line is many of you wonder what is supposed to happen during the offer phase and what your role is supposed to be.

By the time you receive an offer, it should be clear to you whether you want to join the company or organization. You have researched the industry and the company, and you have met with one or several people within the company.

The only reason you would not be able to make a decision is if you are talking with another company or organization and are not far enough along in that process to make a decision. Be honest with the company that you are interviewing with and let them know. Actually, we recommend that you let them know you are pursuing more than one option earlier in the interview process.

Once you receive an offer, your immediate response should be positive, enthusiastic and timely. The response we don't want you to give is, "Thank you. I'll call you back after I've had a chance to think about it." Appropriate responses include:

- Immediate acceptance if you know you want the job. An immediate acceptance demonstrates your excitement and ability to make a decision.
- "Thank you! I'm excited to receive the offer. There are one or two points to the offer I'd like to think through. Is it okay if I call you in the morning (or next business day, if the offer is made on a Friday)?"
- "Thank you. As you know, I am talking with one other company and we have completed the first or second round of interviews." You should be prepared to explain when you expect to know about the other opportunity. If you need to delay an offer acceptance or decline based on another company's interview process timeline, you do run the risk of the company pulling your offer or allowing only a brief period of time to respond.

Accepting an Offer

You've worked and prepared for this moment. You've researched and practiced. You've built and leveraged a network, made personal connections and followed the advice of this book. So when your target company makes you an offer, we expect that you will be prepared to act.

There are three specific things we want you to make sure you do: respond quickly, be enthusiastic and ask for guidance on how you can best or most effectively prepare to start in the new role.

You may be asking yourself, "Is that all?" Well, this is the foundation: you need to demonstrate the clarity and alignment of your intentions, your clear investment in the company and your clear desire for success.

Here's what we mean:

- **Respond Quickly.** This is the first decision you'll make for the company, so be prepared to demonstrate your ability to gather the facts, discuss the details and make a decision. If you are not able to decide quickly, be direct and forthright to your potential employer. If you need time, ask if it's possible to get the time you need. This should not be more than a couple of weeks at the most. Why? Because by this point you should have done your due diligence, you should have a clear sense of the company and you should be ready to make a decision. If you need more time, be sure to talk about why you need more time. It is best if you have previously let the interviewer, or his company, know about your timing and pursuits.

- **Be Enthusiastic.** Be excited about joining the company and show this to your new employer. Your hiring supervisor is most likely equally excited to have you on board. As with any new relationship, your counterpart will want to hear your eagerness about getting started. This does a number of things: reinforces to the hiring manager that he made a good decision; demonstrates this is a good match; makes everyone feel good that they work for a desirable company.

- **Get Started.** You may have heard about a company's onboarding process, which is simply the manner by which they bring in new hires and integrate each into the business. Arrive with ideas about how to quickly settle into your new role. Think through what success will look like for you in the first week, three months and the first year. Ask for guidance, which shows the manager and the company that you are on a mission.

Under-Market Offers

The first question you should ask yourself is simple: is your offer currently under market...or are you seeking more money even though pay is within standards? Your desire to make more money is a difficult negotiating point if you don't have good information to back it up.

If an offer is under-market, it is your responsibility to be credible, thoughtful and fact-based. Referencing college friends, reacting with emotion and eliminating market information from your response will fall on deaf ears.

Instead, rely on data. What does market research reveal about compensation for comparable jobs in comparable companies in the industry? You can find the answer to this question with the help of your career management center, a research librarian and college alumni and corporate recruiters you have met on your campus.

Another way to address this is to consider asking for a three or six-month review that includes setting two or three measurable goals. If you hit your goals, you receive either a one-time cash bonus or a salary increase based on a previously agreed upon number.

Your Counter Offer

Be prepared and organized if you intend to ask to increase an offer. This scenario requires that you to communicate differently than simply receiving a below-market offer. If you plan to counter an offer, do it professionally and respectfully by following "The Three Ps of Offer Negotiation", which are provided to help you walk through the counter offer discussion.

- **Prepare.** Do research to understand your industry's compensation ranges for new college graduates. Think through how this applies to your potential employer and their position in the industry.
- **Probe.** Ask questions to understand the supervisor's and company's objectives as they relate to new college graduate offers. With a base of knowledge, search for common motivators/satisfiers/value propositions.
- **Propose.** Make a prepared and confident counter offer

and keep your mind open to the company's response. Know what you will do based on their potential responses. If their response is to accept or fine-tune your counter, be prepared to accept on the spot. If they are not able to meet your counter or if you are not comfortable with their response, be prepared to decline the offer on the spot. Don't decline an offer as a negotiation tactic. If you decline, be prepared to walk away.

You should know that there are other components of an offer that we believe provide real value to you and your career. While you shouldn't expect to receive the full following spectrum of compensation components, an offer can consist of many pieces: salary, bonus opportunity, signing bonus, equity, benefits, relocation stipend and tuition reimbursement to name a few. Some soft benefits might include continued education such as sales training or internal audit training, as well as retirement fund contributions. Don't be greedy as there are negotiation points to win other than salary and bonus. In communicating through your negotiation, know that self-interests are not attractive to employers. Don't allow your stance on compensation to be solely focused on you. An employer or a recruiter will respond better to you when you frame your questions and interests in terms of their business or client.

Use the following touchstones to guide your thinking about your job offer:

Compensation Ranges

You'll find variability among compensation for similar roles based on company, industry and geography. You'll also find that smaller companies tend to pay based on the person and the skills they bring to bear, where larger companies tend to have "bands" they expect to pay for certain positions and functions. While companies can exceed the pay bands, realize that these pay bands are there for a reason. If you expect to exceed a company's compensation range, be informed, prepared and able to clearly articulate your position.

Pay vs. Experience

High compensation can come at a cost. If a company has an exceptionally high attrition rate, higher pay rates may be offered in order to attract and retain employees. High compensation can also signal heavy commitments to work hours, intensity, travel or required output.

On the other hand, you can gain terrific career experience in lieu of compensation. For instance, can you meet with your company's CEO, CFO or COO on a quarterly or annual basis? If you're in a larger company, this may be a director or vice president. Can you observe an executive team meeting once or twice a year? Can you attend an industry conference? Will your employer pay for or subsidize additional training or education?

Can you have a level of autonomy that allows you to work and go back to school after an agreed to period of time?

Pursue the Intangibles

Are you working for an industry-leading company? Does the company's CEO or executive team have a strong performance track record? Is the company organized to provide you the opportunity to develop a real strength or expertise? Does this company provide opportunity for business travel? What other components exist that add value beyond your personal bottom line?

Exploring Alternatives

Many of the points above are aspects of a new job that could be very attractive to you in the short term. Long term, they can provide perspective, experience and business wisdom that can truly propel you past your peer group. We are not encouraging you to accept a position at below market compensation. We are, however, encouraging you to see a company's value in its entirety before you make a decision, just as with our framing of unpaid internships and the value of experience.

Declining an Offer

The offer discussion is not always smooth and easy. If you

decide to decline an offer, don't create hard feelings. If you find the offer process heading into a negotiation, enter with an appropriate tone. Understand that the negotiation may require you to take a firm stand in communicating your position, view and rationale. However, remember that it is not always what you say, but how you say it.

If you choose to decline the offer or if you are not excited about the offer, speak honestly and professionally with the company representative. To avoid hard feelings, watch your tone, body language and level of interaction while declining the offer, either face-to-face or via phone. Obviously, the offer and negotiation process should be done in person whenever possible, in order to communicate as effectively as possible.

YOUR CHAMPION'S MARGIN TAKEAWAY(S):

_____

_____

_____

_____

_____

_____

_____

_____

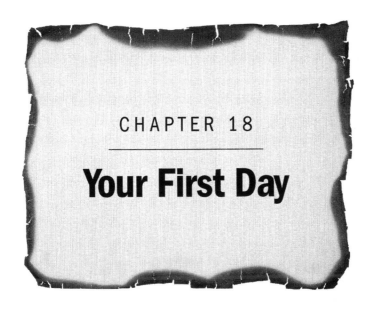

CHAPTER 18

Your First Day

"Whatever you can do, or dream you can do, begin it!
Boldness has genius, power, and magic in it."

—JOHANN WOLFGANG VON GOETHE

CONGRATULATIONS. You received the offer, accepted the job and you're now preparing for your first day. You know it takes a certain focus, effort and preparation to stand out. And we still assume that you went to the trouble of buying and reading this book because you want to identify, pursue and start your professional career on an exciting path. In order to separate yourself from the pack, you will have to be proactive and prepared with a clear head in starting your job and your career.

Some successful individuals will tell you that they were "in the right place at the right time." The secret to real success is being proactive in taking advantage of the opportunities that exist as well as the opportunities that present themselves and the opportunities that you've been creating for yourself throughout reading *Burn Your Resume.* Whatever your situation, we urge you to work harder than everyone else around you. As film mogul Samuel Goldwyn famously said, "The harder I work, the luckier I get."

This chapter offers a template that is designed to help you lay out your proactive plan for the first 100 Days of your new job. This roadmap you create will pave the way for the successful ignition of your career.

Showing Up

Macy's CEO Terry Lundgren once said: "Every morning you wake, you get out of bed, you decide, "Hmm, let's see, on a 1 to 10 scale, what do I want to be today?" We suggest that you begin every day of your the first 100 Days with this mindset.

Your employer may ask you to show up a little later than normal on your first day. He or she may want to get to the office before you in order to prepare to welcome you and begin orientation. However, from day two forward, you will want to arrive at 7:15 a.m., assuming a traditional 8 a.m. business start. You want to send the message that you are eager, dedicated and excited to be there.

You probably won't have a full bill of work on your first few days of work, but there are many value-added things you can do with your "free" time, such as industry research and company research. Regardless of the culture, the role or the location, demonstrating this dedication to your work will positively impact the way co-workers and managers view you.

Be at your desk 30 to 45 minutes before 8 a.m. and 15 minutes after 5 p.m. In some industries, showing up at 7:15 a.m. is too late and leaving at 5:15 p.m. is too early. The bottom line is to show up 45 minutes before the corporate business day starts and stay 15 minutes after the corporate day ends to wrap up loose ends and plan for the next day. You will also find that you get more work done than others who show up for a normal 8 a.m. to 5 p.m. day—as long as you don't waste time or allow others to waste your time. It is absolutely okay to talk with others and we encourage the socialization, but make sure the conversation is relevant and appropriate to your work and the relationship.

Engage Your New Environment

We want you to enter your first day with a plan. In fact, we encourage you to call your manager a full week before your start date to get a sense of the structure you need to develop around your plan. This means that when you talk, you should know or plan to ask specific questions about the following topics:

- What company information can you review before your start date so you can bring ideas on your first day? (There may be private company information not shared during the interview process.)
- Does it make sense for you to meet with colleagues or others in the company during your first day or first week in order to get a sense of where and how you should be directing your time and attention?

- What percentage of your role is customer facing and relationship-based versus being internally focused or an otherwise analytical role?
- Is there competitors' data (or internal analytics) you can review in advance of your start date or that you can have waiting for you on your first day, such as industry data, company data, cultural/market data or cross-functional data?

After you have this conversation with your manager, you should be ready to start making decisions about how you will get started. If information is unavailable prior to your start date, plan to come in early and stay late on the first few days so you can orient yourself as quickly as possible and begin to shape your role and reputation within your new environment. This investment will pay off.

Sir Roger Bannister, an accomplished scientist and the first man to break the four-minute mark in the one-mile run, once said regarding reputation: "Your teammates at school will appreciate it and your professors will respect it. Indeed, everyone with whom you work will know that you are one to count on, and in this shrinking world it is increasingly important to have a positive reputation throughout your network."

In order to be known as "one to count on," you must make conscious choices, decisions and plans, not only about your preparation, but also with regard to your own self-imposed rules about how you'll handle yourself and build your reputation (your "personal brand," as it is popularly known).

Consider the following:

Attire. As we have said: when in doubt, suit up. It is acceptable to ask about dress code, but if you're unwilling to do that you should default to more formal attire. At work, look around to find out how your peers dress, how your boss dresses and how the power-players dress. Make your attire decisions based on those data points. Remember the "+1" concept and dress for the job you want, not the job you have.

Coworkers. Be pleasant. You do not have to be a bouncing ray of sunshine, but take the time to be considerate, pleasant and genuine. You are working to define yourself as a capable and hard-working team player, so act like one and be pleasant to work with.

Be Positive. When we talk about enthusiasm and engagement, we are talking about having a "can-do" attitude. This doesn't imply that you need to be a member of the Sunshine Squad, but it does mean that you should interpret problems as challenges and bring a contagious work ethic to the environment.

Be Productive. Whatever you do with your time, be sure it is productive time spent. Don't waste time showboating, sending emails or leaving voice messages so others know what time you arrived. Use your time to get real work done. Think about current projects and the direction these projects are taking. Plan your day or week or efforts to be effective in your work. Talk with colleagues about the business or talk with people you know outside the company to hear other data points valuable to your work. Your work product and work ethic will be recognized appropriately. This means that when you're early, you should take the opportunity to review company information, get a lay of the land and familiarize yourself with key relationships in the company. Simply speaking, make sure your time is well spent. When in doubt, ask for guidance from your manager about how best to acclimate to the new environment in order to get up to speed as quickly as possible.

Introduce Yourself. Plan to introduce yourself to your team, to the executive assistants in your department and the departments with which you collaborate, and to as many of your peers as is reasonable.

Plan Your First Days. Your calendar may already be set up for you on the first few days. Perhaps there is a formal orientation program that will take one or more days to complete if your company is larger or more established. In these circumstances, be prepared to share a 30- to 60-second sound bite about your new role, your excitement about the company and what you're looking forward to doing most. This will come in handy when you're mixing with current veteran employees. A concrete and contained message will stick in people's heads and offer them a way to file your profile away for later access. This will help you come to mind later when managers are looking to assemble internal teams or are putting taskforces together.

Lunch Expectations. Does your team go out to lunch? Do they eat at their desks? Is it a time that people just and take care of personal "to-do" items? Is this your chance get to know the team or for quality time with your manager or other leaders in the company?

Set Goals. These are questions you need to begin to think about before your start date. It's okay to later refine and revise as you progress through this 1st-100-Days timeline. Plans for your first 30 Days and first 100 Days should have specific items to accomplish. A Day 1 goal might be as simple as "set up voicemail" or "learn intranet system" or "complete new-hire training." A Day 30 goal should be more complex and involve a simple deliverable that will offer empirical evidence of your effectiveness and orientation toward results. Make sure items your goals help you take active and measurable strides toward becoming known as an engaged and productive employee. The learning curve is a costly time for managers and companies, so do everything you can to climb it as quickly as possible. Each day, ask yourself,

"What are the three most important things I can do today to help my project?"

During these first vital days and weeks, be sure to demonstrate positive characteristics, commitment and optimism. For example, whenever someone asks you how your first day is going, be enthusiastic. Nobody wants to be around negativity, even if they razz you for being "green." Everyone wants to think their office is a great one and that they have the best talent, so be open about how excited you are to be here, how it's been great to meet so many new colleagues, or how your team has really gone out of their way to welcome you.

Meet with your manager during your first week to discuss the scope of your role, explicit expectations for performance and clarification for the main goals he or she has for you. When you meet with other leaders in the organization, ask them for input into your role and what they need from you and your projects.

These conversations don't have to be lengthy, but you will find busy managers and executives to be more engaged if they sense you are concise and direct in your questioning. Often, people are willing to help someone who respects their time. Additionally, most people want to think of themselves as experts, so you will be killing two birds with one stone: gaining valuable advice and making power-brokers in your office feel good about themselves. Whether that means having a project timeline for something new you're creating or whether it's a scope-of-work charter, you need to show that you (a) buy into the vision, (b) are independent but a team player and (c) that you are goal-oriented.

YOUR CHAMPION'S MARGIN TAKEAWAY(S):

_____

_____

_____

_____

_____

_____

_____

_____

CHAPTER 19

Leadership: Growing Your Influence

"The key to successful leadership today is influence, not authority."

—KENNETH BLANCHARD

Think ABOUT LEADERSHIP as a toolbox. You need different "tools" to handle different challenges and demands. One size will not fit all situations or leadership opportunities, so you may want to explore your broader skill set prior to any formal interview or formal internship programs.

The following pages feature characteristics of effective leadership types that are commonly characterized under names such as "facilitator," "strategist," "manager," "coach" and so on. We have highlighted the traits and styles that we believe are most important, useful and applicable.

Leadership Types:

Facilitator: Needed to help teams, remove barriers and coordinate activities. This type of leader is an ego-less and quiet facilitator. The Facilitator makes joint decisions with the team as equals, delegating the majority of decisions to the team. This leader is concerned with creating harmony and balance between team members.

Strategist: Sets goals and direction between "big picture" and "ground-level details."

Manager: Responsible for helping everyone understand what needs to be done and making sure tasks are broken up into bite-size tasks. A quality manager has measurable outcomes.

Coach: An experienced, knowledgeable and supportive person who is needed when a team lacks focus, expertise and understanding of what should be done and how. Coaches are concerned with growing people, as well as creating an enabling and trusting environment. This leader makes decisions collectively with a team.

Customer Champion: Someone to empathize and understand how the customer will experience things. Connects strategy with how the customer will see issues.

Commander: These individuals are interested in making decisions. Commanders either make or heavily influence most decisions.

Self-Organization: A cohesive, motivated and confident team doesn't minimal formal leadership. The team makes most decisions, and every member is able to step in to become a leader in specific areas and situations. People are highly capable, committed and self-driven. The team should have diverse and independently thinking team members.

FUNDAMENTALS OF GROUP DYNAMICS:

Group leaders and engaged members need to be conversant in the following practices. Take the time to read and understand the points below so you can practice on your sports teams, student organizations and in-class work groups before arriving at your job or internship.

- Explaining the importance of roles to team success.
  - Can you lead a team? Can you participate as a team member? Do you know when you should take either path?
- High-performance teams: Have you led one?
  - High-performance teams depend on a shared mission, vision and values to align their personal interests, harness their collective expertise and focus their individual effort. They establish clear roles and responsibilities and establish a framework for making decisions and resolving conflicts. Most importantly, they commit to an environment of trust.
  - Members of high-performance teams demonstrate a blend of professional expertise and personal credibility. They hold themselves and each other accountable for the broader impact of their actions foregoing "turf wars." They are skillful, candid communicators, balancing advocacy with openness to others' ideas.

- The best teams perform something akin to "After Action Reviews," which are structured debrief opportunities to reflect on their performance and learn lessons to improve progress and processes. The ability to lead and manage a team's self-analysis is crucial to ongoing success and performance.

Again, these points are a quick and brief summary of group dynamics and the group micro-culture. They are designed to offer you a birds-eye view of your groups' life cycles.

YOUR CHAMPION'S MARGIN TAKEAWAY(S):

_____

_____

_____

_____

_____

_____

_____

_____

CHAPTER 20

Your
100-Day Plan

"The secret of getting ahead is getting started. The secret of getting started is breaking your complex, overwhelming tasks into small, manageable tasks, and then starting the first one."

—MARK TWAIN

Y OUR FIRST 100 DAYS will be over before you know it. By now, you understand that first impressions matter and set the tone for your time in your new job. Indeed, this brief period of "first impressions" will serve to chart your plan through your new company.

As with every other "first" we have discussed in this book, it is easier to start out effectively and powerfully than it is to pull off a turnaround if you get out of position or establish an unsavory reputation. Three months is a healthy timeline to accomplish a great deal, but that time will be gone if you don't plan for it appropriately.

Many books have been written about how to shape your first 100 Days. A favorite is Michael Watkins's book *The First 90 Days: Critical Success Strategies for New Leaders at All Levels.* One of the things that makes Watkins's book such a powerful guide for helping professionals shape their new roles is that it utilizes world-renowned change expert John Kotter's eight-step change process, which outlines the process of aligning resources, expectations, messaging, communications and energy to deliver change to an organization. Watkins presents a similarly logical structure to the approach of establishing credibility and impact in a new role.

FIRST 100 DAYS PLAN

When you're thinking about the First 100 Days in its entirety, you might consider designing weekly blocks of activity or perhaps even weekly themes. Every week, you can spend the before- and after-work time learning about different aspects of your business. This might involve asking for 15 minutes of time with colleagues, managers and executives to get a sense of their role, perspective towards the business and helpful insights they may offer you. You may find some who would like to talk with you about this over lunch. Think back to your days networking for this job. Again, you didn't need to take people to coffee or lunch, you needed to be focused and willing to get the information you were seeking in any environment possible. As you join, be in "sponge-mode" so that you're learning as much as possible. Eventually, you will reach a point where you're meeting with people to share the work you're doing.

Remember, you are laying the foundation for an exceptional career, so approach each day with a purpose and follow through on your commitments. It will pay off.

Accomplishments: Day 1, Month 1 and thereafter

Your First-30-Days and First-100-Days plans should have specific items to accomplish. A Day 1 Goal might be as simple as "set up voicemail" or "involve yourself in the corporate intranet system" or "initiate new-hire training." A 30-Day goal will be more complex and should involve a simple deliverable. Whatever the list includes, make sure they are items that help you take active and measurable strides toward becoming a productive team member. The initial learning curve is a costly time for managers and companies, so do everything you can to climb it as quickly as possible. Dale Carnegie, best known for his best-selling book, *How to Win Friends and Influence People*, once said, "Inaction breeds doubt and fear. Action breeds confidence and courage. If you want to conquer fear, do not sit home and think about it. Get started and get busy."

Throughout these first days and weeks, be sure to demonstrate a positive demeanor and optimism. For example, this might mean that whenever you have the chance to meet someone and they ask you how your first day is going, be enthusiastic. Nobody wants to be around negativity. Everyone wants to think their office is a great one and that they have the best talent, so be open about how excited you are to be here, how it's been great to meet so many new colleagues, or how your team has really gone out of their way to welcome you. You can decide how to brand yourself, so why not do it positively? This day one lays the groundwork for your first week, so start out on the right foot.

Extend invites, request time and get specific and protected time with your manager this first week. Make sure it is an integral part of your plan and that you structure it to deliver specific things such as scope for your new role, explicit expectations for performance and clarification for the main goals he has for you. This goes, too, for your meetings with other leaders in the organization: when you meet with them, ask them for their input into how you can best set succeed in this company and role. This doesn't have to be a lengthy conversation and you will actually find busy managers and executives to be more engaging if they sense you are concise and directed in your questioning. They are willing to help someone who respects their time.

Overview: Days 1-30

The theme for the first month (it will help you to think of this in one-month blocks) is learning. Because you are so early in your career, you can differentiate yourself by bringing structure, intent and vision to the way in which you hit the ground in your new job.

When you're thinking about your first 30 Days, consider designing weekly blocks of activity or perhaps even weekly themes to help you learn the business and become involved. Think of it as creating your own rotational program to flesh out your understanding of the business you've joined. If you can't map the business model, you need to find a new resource or team member who can help you clarify how your company does what it does. This might involve asking for 15-minute time segments with colleagues, managers and executives to get a sense of their roles, their perspectives toward the business and helpful insights they may offer you.

It is important to spend your first 100 Days with your team, your closest colleagues. They serve as your initial coalition to support your growth, influence and success. With your team in place to develop, you will also need to reach out to other centers of influence in your organization. Seek to spend individual time with others to learn about their contributions to the company and their top priorities. As long as you ask questions that are intended to expand and improve your understanding of your employer's main strengths, weaknesses, opportunities and threats, you will be an appealing contact for these colleagues.

You may find some people like to talk about these issues over lunch, but don't believe that lunch is the only time to have a meaningful conversation. Think back to your days networking for this job. You didn't need to take people to lunch—you needed to be focused and willing to get the information you were seeking in any environment possible.

Learn as much as you possibly can all the time. You are laying the foundation for an exceptional career, so approach each day with a purpose and follow through on your commitments.

To Do List: First 30 Days

❑ Complete all administrative and required trainings, tasks and orientation activities.

❑ Learn and make a list of top organizational priorities.

❑ Learn and make a list of top departmental priorities and how your role impacts these priorities.

❑ Make a list of contacts you need to develop across the organization and set up times to meet with them all.

❑ Familiarize yourself with your immediate department teammates

❑ Differentiate short-term, mid-term and long-term goals and then choose one to three short-term goals to accomplish and get started.

Overview: Days 31-60

During your second month, you should be able to turn a corner to become even more productive. Without a plan of attack, the time will slip through your fingers and you'll miss the chance to make yourself known as an action-oriented individual.

By the second month of your employment, you should have already familiarized yourself with the business model, key role-players, members of your team and key actions you can take to make a real impact in your company.

According to Kotter and Watkins, this intermediate time is

best used to achieve, celebrate and communicate small victories. This means completing one or more of your short-term goals, showing progress toward your longer-term initiatives, and being able to share that success with the people around you.

Given that you will be approaching two months of employment, it makes sense to build on that early success by identifying a mentor. A mentor is someone you can observe and learn from, and it is not necessarily a formal relationship. Ideally, you should interact with this person on a daily, weekly or monthly basis, although that is not always necessary. A mentor should be a person of influence in your organization, someone who can teach you from his or her experience and begin to share a more detailed opinion of you and your work, based on his experience. This person can be someone who is only a couple years ahead of you or someone who has 10 to 20 years on you. You may have more than one mentor, too.

To Do List: Days 31-60

- ❑ Find and secure a mentor(s). Remember, you can have multiple mentors and you do not have to formalize these relationships.
- ❑ Recalibrate your goals and volunteer to help someone else with a challenging project.
- ❑ Strengthen rapport with your team through shared interests and activities.

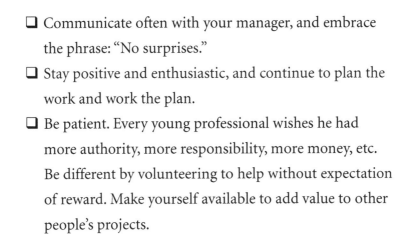

❑ Communicate often with your manager, and embrace the phrase: "No surprises."

❑ Stay positive and enthusiastic, and continue to plan the work and work the plan.

❑ Be patient. Every young professional wishes he had more authority, more responsibility, more money, etc. Be different by volunteering to help without expectation of reward. Make yourself available to add value to other people's projects.

These steps may seem self-evident. If that is the case, you are ready to engage the process quickly without the longer run-up required for young professionals who enter jobs without plans.

Overview: Days 61-100

Plan your work, work your plan. Without a plan and without hard dates by which to deliver them, you will find yourself at the end of this third month without having achieved many goals. Your first 100 days may be hectic, but you only get one change to define your character, work ethic and passion to the organization.

An important piece of your 100-Day plan is achieving something you've promised to deliver to the company. You have already worked through the professional network, identified a potential mentor and earned small or short-term victories that you can celebrate. You have communicated up the chain of command and presented yourself with collegiality in all settings. When anyone asks you how you are doing, you answer with enthusiasm and gusto for your new team, your new role and the organization as a whole. People will want to work with you.

This final month, the final stage of your first 100 Days, is all about action, action, action. By now, you know the centers of influence and you have projects to work on and work to deliver. You might personalize communications to ask for help driving your agenda, securing resources for your tasks, or creating a dynamic in which your ideas are given serious consideration. Obviously, you will need to communicate with leadership from the grassroots of the organization all the way up to at least the executive assistant of the senior leadership team of your company. Find trusted resources and get the message into their hands.

In this action-packed month, you will bring your new teammates and collaborators around your own agenda. Having worked for and with them, they should be willing to offer more of their time and energy to you. This will allow you to manage a project timeline to delivery and to show your ability to align your resources behind something of strategic importance to the organization. This value is consistent across employment settings, whether you find yourself in an early-stage startup or in a stable and old-guard corporation. Your ability to deliver results is the key to your success in this final lap of your first 100 Days.

To Do List: Days 61-100

- ❑ Maintain focus on time and proactive communication.
- ❑ Drive for results on longer-term projects, yours and your teammates.
- ❑ Maintain positivity even in the face of probable set-backs and tension.
- ❑ Continue to invest in relationships—mentors, teammates, centers of influence.
- ❑ Prepare a report for your boss of the work you've completed and impact created during your first 100 Days of employment. Ask for feedback.

By this point you should be getting into a rhythm. You've been working for three months and have reached important milestones, completed important deliverables and seeded important relationships. You will notice that our points speak to the importance of maintaining momentum. Keep the momentum going.

YOUR CHAMPION'S MARGIN TAKEAWAY(S):

_____

_____

_____

_____

_____

CHAPTER 21

The Champion's Margin Checklist

"I believe that the whole career ladder concept is a very
disruptive concept, because what does it suggest? You
can't get past the person ahead of you unless you push
them off the ladder. It promotes aggressive behavior.
When you think of an obstacle course, there are a lot of
people on the obstacle course at the same time, and
my success doesn't impede your success. And I may
be able to take a minute and help you over that next
obstacle and still get where I want to go."

—BARBARA KRUMSIEK

By NOW YOU KNOW that "The Champion's Margin" is a differentiator. It's what sets you apart. It's the small stuff you do to separate yourself, to initiate and develop an exceptional career. In sports, you hear about it all the time: the extra effort, the lean at the race's finish line, the reach for the wall of the pool that yield the fractions of seconds separating first from second, the champion from the runner-up. Achieving The Champion's Margin depends on your work, effort, investment and your willingness to try, fail and try again. Separating yourself from the rest of your peer group requires an unwavering commitment to taking the next step.

The following list is a visual reminder and quick-reference guide for you as you take action to ignite your exceptional career.

THE CHAMPION'S MARGIN

1. Prepare for and meet with your career management center (CMC).

2. Narrow your search to include your natural gifts and talents, passions, strengths, interests, geography and motivations.

3. Don't follow the masses as you work to identify what opportunities exist in your chosen area(s). Ask yourself whose path you are on and who you want to become.

4. Set "Big Hairy Audacious Goals" to drive your first one to three years. Six areas for setting goals: business and career, community, faith, finances, personal (health and relationships).

5. Your resume needs to communicate a purpose within a 30-second glance. Make sure you tell a story that is results-oriented and easy to understand.

6. Your resume and personal story need to be: Clear, Concise, Consistent and Connected (The "4 Cs").

7. Networking is about building and developing personal connections with purpose.

8. Know your entrance: when, where, how and why to introduce yourself. Be brief, be bright, be gone.

9. Take action: make the call, introduce yourself and utilize your network.

10. Know your audience: what they have, what they need and what they like.

11. Interview preparation: You can gather a tremendous amount of information in only 20 minutes.

12. Develop a basic set of fundamental business skills.

13. Plan for interview questions and practice your responses.

14. Your mental attitude and appearance matters (Be and dress "+1").

15. Know your interviewer's hot buttons and what he aims to learn from you.

16. The "feel" of an organization is the simplest way to think about corporate culture.

17. Your post-interview follow-up is a great opportunity to build on your interview. Handwritten thank you notes stand out.

18. Negotiating an offer: Prepare, Probe and Propose.

19. Separate yourself and start your new employment on a strong foundation in your first 100 Days.

20. Be aware of your leadership style. Be able to transition between leading and participating.

21. When in doubt, action wins over inaction. Start your new job as prepared as possible. Make decisions as if you were an owner in the business.

THE FINAL CHAPTER

Ignite!

"Something in human nature causes us to start slacking off at our moment of greatest accomplishment. As you become successful, you will need a great deal of self-discipline not to lose your sense of balance, humility, and commitment."

—H. ROSS PEROT

THE FINAL POINT OF OUR BOOK is the first point in your taking the big step from college to your career. It is very important in making the transition from college student or intern to new professional: be willing to represent the work you're contributing, but be humble enough to ask for suggestions about how to improve it. Every manager wants confident but reflective, productive but receptive, driven but patient young talent. You can be that person—The Champion—by following the suggestions in this book.

With your First 100 Days plan: define who you want to be in this role, identify your goals, plan your action and then execute. As we stated earlier, you are laying the foundation for an exceptional career, so approach each day with a purpose and follow through on your commitments. This may seem overwhelming, but remember what Confucius wisely observed: "Choose a job you love and you will never have to work a day in your life."

Our experience and insights can guide you in your decision making, but know that this book is not the only source for your career development. You can connect with the *Burn Your Resume* community. This will provide further interaction with us and with your peers who are pursuing their goals and sharing their lessons learned and successes. Our advice will help you transition from college to your career and we will provide advice for the next step in your professional life.

After your first several years in the professional world, you will have built and expanded your experiences and developed clarity about your strengths and passions. Most likely, you will be thinking about the next step in your career.

You will find us there, waiting at that intersection, ready to help you reflect on your experience, refine and develop your career path, and take action in further developing your exceptional career.

CONNECT WITH US

Engage with us as you read *Burn Your Resume* and
pursue your career. We have created an online community
for you to engage with us and with your peers.

www.BurnYourResume.com
http://www.Facebook.com/BurnYourResume

You can also contact us directly:
Paul@BurnYourResume.com
Ethan@BurnYourResume.com